Otto Preminger is one of the American
cinema's most eminent figures. From
dramatic entertainments like Laura
and Anatomy of a Murder to films
touching the larger issues of the post-
war world like Exodus and Advise and
Consent, he has proved his thoughtful-
ness and versatility. This lively guide
to his work has been compiled by Gerald
Pratley, the distinguished Canadian
film critic.

The Cinema of
Otto Preminger

$2.95   90p

In the same series,
produced by THE TANTIVY PRESS
and edited by Peter Cowie:

The Cinema of

OTTO PREMINGER

by
Gerald Pratley

The International Film Guide Series

A. ZWEMMER
LONDON

A. S. BARNES & CO.
NEW YORK

ACKNOWLEDGEMENTS

The author and publishers wish to thank Otto Preminger for his kind help in the compilation of this volume, including the supply of stills, script pages, and other information. Also his assistant, Nat Rudich, and Saul Bass & Associates Inc., who supplied the original artwork pulls of several of their famous Preminger title logos. Finally, thanks are also due to the Ontario Film Institute, and the Canadian Broadcasting Corporation.

Cover design by Stefan Dreja

FIRST PUBLISHED 1971
Copyright © 1971 by Gerald Pratley
Library of Congress Catalog Card No. 74–141573
SBN 302 02152 3 (U.K.)
SBN 498 07860 4 (U.S.A.)
Printed by C. Tinling and Co Ltd, London and Prescot

I live in the United States. I originally was born in Vienna, and lived there a long time. In the United States, one of the most precious rights we have is the right of free expression. I have had trouble with censorship, with the small movie, *The Moon Is Blue*, because in 1953 people objected to the word "virgin," which is hard to believe. I could have easily made a few cuts and compromised, but I feel that in our own fields, as motion picture directors, newspapermen, writers, whatever we are, we have not only the right, but the duty to defend this right of free expression; because if this right deteriorates, that is the first step to dictatorship, to totalitarian government, and no totalitarian government, whether on the Right or on the Left, could ever exist with its citizens having the right to speak freely. I think it is very important for us to fight for this right and that is why I have always fought censorship and won. There is no censorship in the United States. I hope it will stay like this. That is my answer to questions about censorship. My views have never changed.

Otto Preminger,
Ontario Film Theatre,
Toronto, October 1970.

Shooting PORGY AND BESS. Preminger at extreme left

THE FILMS OF OTTO PREMINGER

First Period

Second Period

PART ONE

In Austria Vienna, 1931

An "exciting city of gaiety and romance," of music, art and aristo-
cracy. Among the legion of pretty girls hoping to make their name in
the theatre and to succeed under Reinhardt was an eighteen year-old
from Budapest, daughter of a Baron, who had just graduated from
the University of Vienna. Her stage name was Marion Mill and so
far she had done quite well in revues. On returning from a holiday in
Venice she was sued by a night club owner for breach of contract.
Terrified at the thought of court appearances and publicity which
would distress her family, she sought advice from an older friend,
Kitty Hoffman, who knew Vienna well, asking her to suggest a
lawyer, trustworthy and not too expensive.
Miss Hoffman, realising that a lawyer involved in the theatre would
be more sympathetic to her case than one from the "outside" world,
sent her to a young assistant director in one of Reinhardt's theatres
who also happened to be a doctor of law. She called him "a genius,"
extremely talented in the theatre and extremely clever in other
matters. His name was Otto Preminger.

Preminger settled the action against Miss Mill, gave her a part in
The Front Page, which he was directing, and a year later, married her.
At this time, as a young man, he had already experienced the sweet-
ness of success, but not without having worked hard to achieve it.
He was learned, witty and widely-read, and could quote at length
from Goethe, Shakespeare and Roman Law. His finesse in directing,
in acting and in conversation was so great that Reinhardt, whose
stature was then almost legendary and god-like, paid attention to
him far beyond that he accorded his other actors and directors, and
usually gave him the freedom to work in his own way.

Hollywood, California, 1943
[20th. Century-Fox Studios]

Zanuck left the Army and came back to the studio. He and Bill Goetz (who had taken his place) had a tremendous falling-out, Zanuck didn't even come to the studio until Goetz had left physically; but he had taken over again, and one day I got a call to go to his house on the beach, and he still remembered we had had that damn fight over *Kidnapped*. I still remember the scene: Zanuck owned this beautiful house on the beach at Santa Monica, and on entering you walked through the living-room. The butler took me to the pool, and Zanuck sat at the pool with his back to me. The butler said: "Mr. Preminger is here," but Zanuck didn't rise, or offer me a seat or anything. Speaking tersely, he said: "You're working on several properties. I think two of them, *Army Wives* and *Laura*, are not bad. You can produce them. As long as I am at the studio, you will *never direct*. Goodbye." I was dismissed like an errand boy.

Otto Preminger

Baton Rouge, Louisiana, November 1966
[On location, *Hurry Sundown*, St. Gabriel's Prison Farm]

Bert and Katya Gilden both wore sun helmets. They looked as though they had started out on safari to Africa and, not long after, had got lost in Louisiana. There they stood, looking somewhat forlorn and neglected, in the midst of this intense activity which meant their book was being made into a film. Although they were the authors, their creation appeared to have been taken away from them, and they now seemed to be the last to have anything to do with the enterprise. This was true, as it is of all authors who surrender their work (after generous payment, usually), to the film-maker. For fourteen years he had worked in New England factories, she had kept house and raised three children, and during this time they had, in the

9

evenings, worked together and written a book. Its title; *Hurry Sundown*.

"Hurry sundown, see what tomorrow bring . . ."
from the songs that Rose Scott used to sing

St. Gabriel's Prison Farm, once a place of incredible hardships for its inmates, mostly Negroes, is miles from civilisation. The noise was deafening, although when scenes were being filmed, all was quiet. The moment the camera stopped, earth-moving equipment went to work building a lake, to be used for the climax of the film; explosives were planted, air-conditioning trucks lumbered around, trucks drove up with new supplies, buses and cars, used to transport the unit, moved from place to place. Clouds of dust hung in the air, the heat was paralysing, generators hummed providing power, and thick cables snaked in all directions. Over two hundred unit workers and technicians either stood around or moved equipment, and set up the next scene. Everyone seemed exhausted by the heat, flies and fraying tempers. Trailers housing the stars stood alongside large trucks holding electrical equipment, props, costumes and camera gear. One worker walked over to a portable water dispenser, filled the small plastic cup, rinsed his mouth and spat out the water on the parched, down-trodden grass.

At that moment the great Preminger appeared on the scene, as if from nowhere. Pointing at the man he shouted, in his European-accented English, "How dare you! Get out of my sight, leave this location. Your manners are abominable, your work is deplorable. I will not have such filthy behaviour on my set. You are fired. Leave."

The man took his coat and slunk away through the bushes. With everyone else wilting in all directions, Preminger strode up a hill with unflagging energy to speak to Michael Caine, who was to drive an old Cadillac down the hill to the house of John Phillip Law. Here, Jane Fonda, carrying her small child, was to run into the scene. The difficulty was that Caine didn't drive, and he pretended to do so as the car ran down the hill. He was required to stop it on the marks, and

Faye Dunaway, Diahann Carroll, and John Phillip Law in HURRY SUNDOWN

John Phillip Law was to walk over to speak to him. It was a long and difficult take. Then John Phillip Law kept fluffing his lines.

"Mr. Law," roared Preminger, "it is too hot to take this scene forty times. Will you remember your lines." The chickens had by now been over-fed and wouldn't "come on scene" when called. The children would not co-operate. Striding through the carnage like a general on the battlefield, Preminger, who is not a young man, bellowed them all into line, chickens and children alike. Taking off his sun helmet and mopping his bald head, he called his assistant director.

"Burt," he yelled, "why must you complicate my life, why cannot I depend on you? Get that cow out of the field, it wasn't there before."

The sun burned down, the offending cow was removed, the chickens came back, Mr. Law remembered his lines, Mr. Caine drove splendidly, the long crane shot was completed. Preminger went tramping gamely back up the hill to prepare his next scene.

Preminger has the reputation of being a difficult man, rude, heartless and impatient. He becomes this way when people do not follow his instructions. Otherwise he is direct, outspoken, but never hostile. He detests insincerity, stupidity and gush. He is a colourful character who says exactly what he thinks, and expects the people who work for him to do their tasks quickly, efficiently and well. Watching some films being made, it is difficult to know who the director is and to discover where he is. This is not the case with Preminger. Not only is he seen everywhere, he can be heard a mile away.

Making *Hurry Sundown* was not easy, and the heat didn't help. It was so hot that everyone ran with perspiration and tempers were short. More than this, there hung over the production the atmosphere of resentment on the part of the white community which objected to the film being made here.

The night before a policeman had met me at New Orleans airport with instructions to drive me to the hotel in Baton Rouge. He had delivered the exposed film for that day to be air-mailed to the Paramount studios in Hollywood for processing.

He might have stepped out of a Preminger picture. His belly hung over his belt, his gun was stuffed carelessly into its holster, his shirt was rumpled and creased and he sweated profusely. Hollywood's so-called stereotypes are disturbingly true to life. His police cruiser was filthy. He eased himself behind the wheel and started on the drive to St. Francisville. He reached under the seat and brought out a plug of tobacco, saying, "Mah wife don't like me to chew at home so I make up for it on these here drives and while on duty." With a savage gesture he sounded the car horn at a Negro driver, who, said the policeman, was going too slow in the lane ahead of him. "All the

Faye Dunaway and John Phillip Law in HURRY SUNDOWN

accidents," he said, "are the fault of the niggers on the road."

The former "white" and "coloured" signs on the restaurants and shops had disappeared. "Don't worry about that," he said. "Nothing's changed. Do you think we are going to let the niggers use our toilets? Would you want to sit on a toilet used by a black? We've got ways of taking care of this. We ain't got nothing against the niggers. They know their place down here, we keep them in it and there ain't no trouble. To them, I'm king. I patrol around the town and I take care of them." He gave a knowing look.

"But when these outside folks come here to make trash like this movie, then there's always trouble. The fine people of Louisiana are real upset by this film." He mused for a while and continued "The

Fonda girl was actually seen kissing the nigger man." He sweated and leered at the thought of it, saying, "The townspeople won't stand for sich things."

The man in question was Robert Hooks, who was keeping a diary of his days in Louisiana. "You can feel the eyes watching you behind the curtains," he said. One property man went to the laundromat to dye some towels for Diahann Carroll's bathroom scene in the film. He was chased out by a man shouting, "Get out of here with those niggah towels." Miss Carroll, who rarely journeyed out after dark, said: "You can cut the hostility with a knife. I'm not a fighter, I usually smile and then go to my room and cry my eyes out." Attitudes ranged from unfriendly—the Negro players were rarely served in local restaurants and ate mainly in their rooms—to condescending. Rex Ingram was spoken of as "Uncle Remus."

Finally the day ended and as the sky darkened the unit fled the advancing mosquitoes and retreated to the showers, swimming pools and air-conditioned rooms of the Bellmont in Baton Rouge, a colonial-style motel with a Confederate flag flying high, and a reputation for hospitality to movie people. The Negro players found little of it, especially after it was learned that Preminger was making a film about "niggers getting the best of the whites." The place was guarded by soldiers as though it were an armed camp.

When Preminger made *Carmen Jones* and *Porgy and Bess*, in which Diahann Carroll also played leading roles, he never went near any of the southern states. Times and movies have changed and Preminger today makes all his films on location. The setting of *Hurry Sundown* is Georgia, but Preminger found it impossible to make the picture there. After great difficulty he finally obtained permission to film in Louisiana, around Baton Rouge and a small town called St. Francisville. The townspeople were anything but sympathetic.

"This is Otto all over again," said an unkind acquaintance. "Anything for publicity." But, to Preminger's credit, he refused to discuss the situation. It is not true that Preminger creates so-called controversy in order to capitalise on it. "People object to what I do because I try to find the truth, and in many cases, the truth is not pleasant. They are afraid of it."

New York City, 1970
[711 Fifth Avenue]

From Vienna to New York, across forty years of cinema; in some ways Otto Preminger is not the same man at all. Physically he looks different, and changing languages changes a person. He has worked for more years in English than he did in German; but spiritually he is the same, remaining true to his beliefs and living up to his standards. His life has been varied, full and active, and lived in many different places, encompassing the "old" world and the "new," ranging from the Thirties to the Seventies, from Vienna's theatres to 20th. Century-Fox's sound stages, and covering an era of achievement peopled by artists, technicians and impresarios, some of whom have faded into movie and theatrical history. It has been a lifetime of effort through which Preminger has battled great storms and emerged triumphant as his own master in a house usually owned by others.

At the present time, he occupies a spacious suite of offices on the top floor of the Columbia Pictures head office on Fifth Avenue. Although surrounded by formality, he is accessible to almost everyone; a commanding and authoritative figure—he would have made an excellent general in any army—yet friendly, courteous and sympathetic. He cannot be deceived, manipulated, or exploited. He is outspoken, honest, and always to the point in his opinions and conversation. He is precise, tidy, punctual, immaculately dressed and well-groomed at all times. Yet he is never insufferable over these traits because his life is filled with intent and achievement. His sense of humour, his engaging use of English, his colourful and dynamic character, make him a constantly entertaining figure. Above all, he is a man of keen intelligence with a shrewd and knowing insight into other people. He can also breathe fire and brimstone in spectacular amounts when those under his direction are not doing what he asks.

The office is decorated mainly in black-and-white. The black, solid, silent door, with OTTO PREMINGER on the wall in the familiar Saul Bass-designed white lettering, looks forbidding; but once on the other side the interior is light, cool, pleasing and modern. Lining the hall are posters of his films—those made since he became an independent producer.

Inside his large corner office, with windows filling two sides, Otto Preminger sits at a long, elegant marble-top table, again white on black. The seats—his own and those for secretaries, assistants and visitors—are black, comfortable swivel armchairs. They put a person at ease immediately. There is a long, restful divan, a table for conferences, book cases, and a splendidly outfitted washroom. His desk-table contains only work of an immediate nature, but the low shelves behind are filled with books, screenplays and miscellaneous volumes. The modern paintings on the walls are by Diego Rivera. There are telephones within easy reach of almost every sitting position, but only one on his desk—the kind which can be talked into without lifting the receiver, while the voice of the caller is heard on a speaker. His calls are so numerous that to be forever picking up the receiver would become wearying. For confidential calls, however, he presses the button which cuts out the speaker and then uses the receiver. He is in constant communication with his wife by direct line to his home on Sixty-fourth Street and calls four or five times a day to inquire about her and the two children (a twin son and daughter). He asks about his wife's work—preparing French subtitles for *Junie Moon* (Preminger was dissatisfied with those on the print shown at Cannes).

A day in the life of Otto Preminger (when he is not away filming) is not far removed from what we have come to accept through journalism and movies as the caricature of the busy executive. It is part carnival, comedy, tragedy and triviality, with Preminger as the ringmaster remaining bemused and benevolent (some of the time) at the centre, genuinely trying to direct hopes, ambitions and schemes into some productive pattern of accomplishment; while, at the same time, trying to pursue his own future plans.

This particular morning finds him in conversation with Nat Rudich, his knowledgeable production assistant and general adviser for the past fourteen years. "Why is it that Hope [Mrs. Preminger] can speak to him but he cannot return the calls on the direct line?" Rudich has spoken to the telephone company and explains with technical precision and maps where the complicated cable system has gone wrong. The company was working on it immediately (visions of scores of workers going down into manholes came to mind), but Preminger doubted that it was immediate enough.

The regular phone line, however, was ringing constantly.

"Yes, this is Otto Preminger."

A young, eager, female voice: "Mr. Preminger, I am calling for the Film Industry for Peace in Vietnam Committee, and we plan to stop work one day next month to express our disapproval of the Government's policy on Vietnam. Would you join us?"

"Who are 'us'?"

(Eager voice recites the names of well-known directors and stars.)

"Well, you see, I am not actually working. I'm working but not filming. I could ask my staff and myself (there are six of us here) to stay home but who would know, who would care? This is hardly the dramatic gesture you have in mind. But I am in sympathy with your beliefs so please send me your letterhead and aims and objects, and I will get in touch with you."

"Thank you, Mr. Preminger."

In quick succession come calls from a young writer with a screenplay he would like Mr. Preminger to read; a vague friend of a friend calling to ask if Mr. Preminger will read his book; a producer from San Francisco who wants Preminger to see his play; a film-maker who wants Preminger to see his first film. Preminger replies that he will be in California in a few days and arranges to see him; a lady who thinks that Preminger is a form of directory assistance, asks where to reach a number of other film personalities. He patiently tells her. To others who want to send him various things, or to visit him, he spells out his address and other details.

17

Frank Sinatra calls. Preminger would like to film *The Godfather*, but only if Sinatra will appear as the "Godfather." He would prefer not to. Their conversation is long and friendly. C.B.S. calls. They would like to use Liza Minnelli on a special show. Where can she be found? Preminger suggests Vincente Minnelli's home. She was staying there. A producer from Rome is on the line. He wants to talk about a co-production. Preminger is not interested. He does not co-produce. His work is his own entirely.

Always a thoughtful and considerate host, Preminger asks one of the girls in the office to bring in coffee, which she does, in china cups. Preminger will have nothing to do with plastic containers. As she leaves she mentions that Mr. X is waiting outside for his eleven o'clock appointment. Preminger explains why Mr. X is here: "You know that my next film will be *Such Good Friends*. This gentleman is a composer and he tells me he has written a title song for me and he wants me to hear it."

Mr. X enters. He is obviously a salesman and his product is himself. He is brash, talkative and supremely self-confident. He walks briskly to the table sits down at one end and brings out a small portable tape-recorder. As he fits it up he reels off the names of composers and other artists who have praised his work. As the music begins he sings to it. He goes through several choruses of lyrics ending with a great burst of voice and music straining to the climax with "that is why we are such good friends." The song has hardly died away before the author is describing why it is so good and so right for Preminger, who thought he could detect references to other tunes in the music. It also sounds like the Thirties, thinks Preminger. The composer is affronted.

"Do you think you could use it?"

"Frankly no. I don't like it."

The composer argues with Preminger, who replies: "You ask me if I like it. I tell you no."

Packing up his equipment, the song-writer leaves.

Preminger shrugs. Rudich comes in to say the trailer for *Junie*

Moon is ready to look at in the Columbia screening room several floors below. On the way down, Preminger discusses the rating given it, and where it will be placed on the print.

A walk to the Algonquin Hotel follows where Preminger is to be interviewed on a radio programme with Marjorie Kellogg. In the room-cum-studio he greets her affectionately and then sits down looking benign and helpful.

Only the innocent interviewer would be unaware, however, that whenever Preminger is interviewed, the first coy and perhaps silly questions will get impatient answers. "Ask me anything you want," he will say, but there is no question Preminger hasn't heard a hundred times before, and he starts to answer before the question is half-way through. But from the most trivial queries he can fashion the most brilliant answers on any subject, person, place or current event. Like Jean Renoir, he has the gift of giving broad answers to the narrowest questions. He can also be very funny.

With the half-hour over, Preminger goes to lunch, where several acquaintances join him at the table with Nat Rudich. The conversation centres on the opening of *Catch 22* and the announcements and references to its enormous budget, prompting Preminger to remark that "it does not pay, as I have always said, to talk about what a film costs." Everywhere he walks, he is greeted alike by friends and strangers; he is part of an envied fraternity.

His assistant, Eric Kirkland, a pleasant and intelligent young man, starts the afternoon by coming in with a script. It is the dialogue of *Junie Moon* taken from the soundtrack on a movieola. Preminger has discovered an error which could mean a faulty translation in other languages. He is highly displeased, asks for an explanation, and then makes it clear that he will not tolerate mistakes such as this. But his anger is confined to the issue in question, and the next time Eric enters, Preminger will greet him warmly and without prejudice.

Rudich enters to report that a friend has gone to hospital. "He is the bearer of bad news," says Preminger. "He knows everyone who has the stroke. Bring us some good news."

*Raf Vallone and Tom Tryon (back half turned to camera) in THE
CARDINAL*

Now, four men with cameras and sound equipment arrive. They
are from Holland. A director, an interviewer, a cameraman and a
sound engineer. They have come to interview Preminger for Dutch
television. Preminger is very obliging, but tells them firmly to watch
his paintings and not damage them. The director, a tall young man,
outlines the procedure. Preminger is to walk in smiling, take a turn
around his office and seat himself at his desk. They rehearse and shoot
it several times. Preminger keeps up a string of comments about film-
making ending by saying: "Everyone in Holland will know that he
directed Otto Preminger!" He begins to answer the familiar questions.

The home telephone line is working and he talks to his wife, whom he affectionately refers to as "Hopesy." He is to arrange for his son's trunk to be picked up. He is going to a summer camp. She has been to the dentist with the children. There is nothing to worry about.

Nat Rudich returns. He has been studying the original contract for *The Cardinal* to see what television conditions are set out and on what terms with Columbia. A law suit appears to be in the offing. To Preminger, it is going over past work, which finished when the picture was completed. It is tiresome but necessary. "You are late," he tells Rudich, "and you have no news."

It is six o'clock and Preminger is going home for dinner. With traffic conditions being what they are in New York City he does not own or drive a car, preferring to walk between his home and office, a good ten minute stretch. Proceeding along Fifth Avenue and across to Sixty-fourth Street he proves again to be the living evidence of the power of television. Although he is never seen in his own films and does not have the Hitchcock figure and image, he is as well-known as Hitchcock as a result of his numerous appearances on late-night television interview programmes. With his distinctive voice and appearance (his bald head always visible among the crowds) he is constantly being hailed and greeted, welcomed and asked for his autograph, from the respectful attendant at Cartier's (where he went to pick up Mrs. Preminger's watch) to garbage collectors passing by in their huge truck labelled SAVE WATER, who waved and called out "Hello Otto." He waved back and acknowledged other greetings, always with dignity and never making an exhibition out of such behaviour. A student approached and addressed him by name asking him to buy a raffle ticket in the cause of a movement against the use of drugs. He bought one expressing respect for the many students concerned with social responsibilities. A blind Negro beggar stood on the corner, a tin can around his neck. "If a man has to sink to this level to live," said Preminger, "then he deserves a coin whether he is genuine or not."

Preminger walks quickly through the crowds and is a fascinating conversationalist. He keeps up a steady observation about life and people, with many amusing and serious stories about himself and events which have befallen him during his career. His house is tall and narrow, double locked and hard to enter. The *décor* is similar to and in the same colours as the office. Dinner is served quietly on a round transparent table in a room of striking simplicity and modernity, lit by concealed lighting, adorned with several impressive sculptures and paintings. Through a picture window at the end of the long room, a Henry Moore sculpture, bathed in a beam of light, stood in silent solitude in a small, gravelled garden, surrounded by shrubs and a high fence lost in the gathering darkness.

On the top floor, reached by a small lift, Otto Preminger has built a screening room. With numerous telephones, gadgets of all kinds, and a control panel which pulls out like a drawer from the table in front of a long sofa, the room is an electronic delight, which Preminger finds pleasing to demonstrate to visitors and to use himself. The screen comes down over the window, the projection ports open in the wall. High cupboards contain copies of his scripts and some of his films. But little else it seems.

He does not think very much about the past nor store away in his mind very many details about his work. Many of his early films he refuses to discuss. They are over and done with. If any of them live on in cinema history, naturally he is pleased. "But it is for you (the critics) to analyse them if you want to, to discuss themes, styles and meanings."

PREMINGER—An Appreciation

At a time when most directors call themselves "independent," the only American film-maker who comes close to achieving such an ideal working condition is Otto Preminger, the man who originally started the independent movement away from the major studios*. The reason for this is simple to explain, but not easy for others to achieve: he asserts complete control over everything he does and never relinquishes it until his films are out of distribution. Even then, the pictures remains under his jurisdiction. It is interesting to look back over the years and see that the absolute control which Zanuck once held over Twentieth Century-Fox and every film-maker who worked for him (including Preminger – and in the end responsible for Preminger striking out on his own) has now been achieved by Preminger, the important difference being that this control is only over himself and not over that of others. Preminger is a dictator in that he is a law unto himself with his own work, is answerable only to himself, and performs all the functions necessary to prepare, produce, direct and then show his films.

Most artists, once they have completed what might be termed the creative part of their labours, are content to turn their finished work over to the mechanical processes that have been set up over the years to bring it to the public. The writers give their manuscripts to the publisher to be printed, confident that once accepted their books will not be cut or re-edited at a later date because they are not selling well, or falsely advertised or sent to back-street bookshops if the reviews prove indifferent. The composer gives his work to the symphony orchestra knowing that it will not be re-titled or shortened

* To say this is not to overlook such veteran independents as Hunt Stromberg, Benedict Bogeous, Walter Wanger, Edward Small, and others who released through UA in the Forties, or Samuel Goldwyn and Walt Disney, who created their own studios.

to fit a double bill of two major works; and the playwright, once his play has been finally staged, opened and running, knows that subject to the skills of various acting companies, it will remain as he wrote it. Painters and sculptors know that exhibitions of their work will not be touched up or chipped about by gallery owners hoping to make it more palatable for the public.

The film-maker alone experiences the frightening dismay of seeing his work changed because the distributor has other ideas. The huge financial outlay required to make even an average film (which is not required by other artists) means that as the film-maker cannot pay for it himself, he is at the mercy of the financiers if his work is deemed unacceptable for the public. Even more galling is the knowledge that the men who change their work have no way of knowing that they are making it acceptable for large audiences.

Every film-maker knows that while he may be in complete control during pre-production and shooting and may even be using the actors he thinks best suited to the parts without regard for "box-office" names, the day comes when the finished print must be handed over to the men who paid the piper. Everyone then dances together with joyful anticipation of a bright and prosperous outcome, or the air is chilled with a bleak acceptance and the director is out in the cold. Once the print is handed over, few directors have anything to do with final editing, the advertising, or the showing of their films. Some may make personal appearances, but most prefer to move on to another film (if they have the backing) rather than wait out the delay between the completion of a film and its first opening. Few want to have anything to do with a picture once they have finished it, finding the "selling" part of it tedious and non-creative.

It is against this background that Preminger must be set and considered, and which shows him to be different from his other "independent" colleagues. He has his own headquarters from which he runs himself. He is not afraid to be an artist who works from an office. Here his films are conceived, written, planned, budgeted, cast, negotiated with a distributor (Preminger is not a man to go to other men's offices), given a distinctive design for advertising, a release date, a publicity campaign. To this office come the writers for consultations, the actors for rehearsals, the technicians for planning. All is made ready by Preminger himself. By now his film is firmly implanted in his mind; visually he "sees" what he must do to create what his imagination has conceived in script form. Although he takes no writing credit, he has worked consistently with his writer during the six months he normally takes to prepare the script. The following six months are spent shooting and editing, and in this way he makes a film approximately every year.

What he will not reveal is how much his films cost, what financial arrangements he has made with his distributor, and how much profit was made or money lost on any of his productions. When the time comes for Preminger to send in his finished film, he knows it will remain his film, the way he has completed it. There will be no cuts or compromises for friends or foes, no changes and no rotten advertising. He has seen to everything, even the trailer, the pocket book edition, and the soundtrack recording. Nothing has happened or will happen that was not initiated or approved by him. Everything bears the unmistakeable imprint of Preminger's integrity, force and power. For this reason, because of his total involvement in what so many people term "the business" or "marketing of films" he is often called a businessman in films rather than the artist in the cinema. To this, Preminger will reply that it is all art and creativity, and the process of placing his work before audiences is just as relevant as the creation of the film. To leave out the after-work is to deny the completion of the whole.

When Preminger has finished a film there is no period of waiting, no indecision, no wondering whether a producer will invite him to direct a film, as is the lot of many "independents." Preminger has already selected his next subject, and the vital process of being involved and starting work again begins once more, and in which he fully accepts the responsibilities of freedom.

In studying Preminger's films it is impossible to ascribe to him many of the qualities which are thought to make other directors great artists. It is always easy to categorise, analyse, and applaud the work of directors who stay within a certain style of form, content and expression. A great many American and British directors are given much less than their due because they move over a wide variety of topics, none of which can be readily identified as being their own personal expression of a given theme or subject. Because of this, however, many of them have lasted much longer than those who are considered "personal" and who unfortunately played one theme for so long they fell from grace and favour with critics and audience alike.

Speaking of his independent period, it is useless to ask Preminger why he decided to make any of the films he did. To him, this is asking the obvious. As he is not a hired director any longer, as he chooses the stories himself, it must be because they are of interest to him. This is the only criteria he acknowledges. He does not repeat himself, he enjoys being different; he must be held, interested, moved and excited by the subject he chooses to film. If certain stories and their characters involve him, if their point of view, their actions, their morality, their behaviour, are recognisably that of human kind, whether commendable or reprehensible, and are an expression of social conduct and of events which concern him and society, then he will want to film them. It may be a simple or an elaborate story, it does not matter as long as it has relevance to him. He will not film any subject he does not believe in, nor show events that cannot be recognised as being possible and believable, nor depict people who are not credible, no matter how good or bad their character may be. The results are personal expressions of society seen through best-selling novels, plays and little-known books, and his impassive gaze belies the poignant profundities to be found in his moody studies of perverse psychology.

Preminger's work is eclectic reflecting his catholic taste in literature, art and all human pursuits. (The only kind of film he has not made is a Western, most of which, he feels, have distorted the history of their times.) This being so, it is possible to find in his films all the

Preminger on location with Paul Newman during the making of
EXODUS

themes found only singly in other directors' work: obsession in love and greed for power; politics in government and big business; discrimination and alienation among individuals and groups; the fight for liberty in the physical, legal and personal sense; feminine mystique and male mythology, shown in their true light; war and peace, love and hatred, psychological and social values, imaginative interpretations to well-known events; the deeper levels of thought and communication; all have been explored, depicted and expressed in clean, clear and disciplined statements. Preminger is a realist who brings objectivity to all his work. Obscurantism is for those who lack the freedom to make open statements, or for those who are unable to make clear what they want to say. Subjectively, Preminger shows much of himself without realising it, as do all true artists, and without talking about himself. His work never reflects tiredness or boredom on his part because he never concerns himself with matters which do not interest him or engage his energies to the utmost.

There is no noticeable pictorial style to his films and working with different cameramen doesn't change the look of his pictures. Preminger's reality is the rough and ready look of real places. He does not look for the poetic scene, the eye-filling expanse, the carefully composed landscape or manicured frame. He is on location and what he shows is the way the place is and regretfully, as we look for beauty, we must accept the fact that the world is an ugly place and Preminger isn't going to beautify it for us by spending weeks composing the rare view of the commonplace in man and nature. He would not spend the money, for one thing, which is the main reason why he continues to work steadily while others fall behind. The way places are when he shoots his film is the way he presents reality. For Preminger, it came out better in black-and-white than in colour, but this is not to deny the effectiveness of his world on film, the principal strength of his total quest for objectivity and his commendable detachment emotionally from issues which concern him.

Although Preminger is a very public man he is a very private person. He will not admit that one film was a success, another a failure. He is modest about triumphs and accepts rejection. He does what he feels is right, to the best of his ability, and once done, nothing changes it and there are no excuses. There is no doubt that he was disappointed by the poor critical and public response in North America to *Junie Moon*, which, as with so many films today, prompts the distributor to shelve them rather than to continue showing them thus denying audiences elsewhere the chance to make up their own minds and reverse the domination of New York. He really felt that *Junie Moon* would be accepted as he had accepted and believed in the story and its people. It had become part of him, but the situation does not obscure the fact that *Junie Moon* represents Otto Preminger at his best. He is America's most enduring film-maker, the most individual and independent of them all, and in many ways the most constructive, practical and instinctive at work today.

Everything he is as a man, his artistry, humanity, integrity and skill are all to be found in his beautifully-made films. The way society acts, changes, suffers and seeks freedom in all things is the theme of his work. In this he has presented us with a consistent and rewarding insight into humanity, showing reality and optimism in a profoundly evocative chronicle of events.

After dinner in his screening room

I very early developed a desire to become an actor. My father was a lawyer in Vienna and had an office that doesn't exist any more: Attorney-General for the Austrian Empire. But after the revolution when Austria became a republic, he became a lawyer. A very well-known lawyer. It's strange that when remembering certain incidents from youth, they often become disconnected. One of the things I remember is that he had a client, a very famous actress—she might still be alive for all I know. Her name was Leopoldine Konstantin and she was very beautiful. She was not really his client. The client was the man with whom she lived. He was a big industrialist, a money-man, from Germany who had various troubles and needed representation. His name was Hugo von Lustig. I remember they came often to our house on social visits, and at the age of nine I auditioned for her. At that time, very early, I learned the classics, poems, plays, everything by heart. It was a great moment in my life. She was very kind. It was just to see if I had talent. My father was very wise. We had a wonderful relationship really, like two brothers. He never punished me. There were times when I didn't go to school for many weeks, and when it came to light, he stood up for me, and told the school I really was sick and gave me a chance to catch up what I had missed. I was a little early in school, and I was supposed to go to college, but I wanted to become an actor. When this became evident,

---

*Preminger was born on December 5, 1906.

at the age of sixteen–seventeen, my father talked to me saying he doesn't know anything about acting, nobody in our family had wanted to act, but naturally if I made up my mind, he's not going to be in my way. But if I wanted to do him a personal favour, would I just finish any kind of formal study? As he was a lawyer, I decided I would finish law school. The practice was to go to the university for four years to study law and then to become a lawyer, to work with a lawyer—that's the Viennese or the Austrian way, or used to be. But even before I studied law I started acting. The system in Germany and in Austria is that people who want to become actors don't necessarily stay, let's say in Vienna, waiting to have a chance. There are many repertory companies all over Germany and Austria and you try to enlist in one of them. I didn't do this immediately—I first auditioned while I was still in school for Max Reinhardt, and his main theatre was not in Austria, it was in Berlin. He started an additional theatre in Vienna. A very rich man, he always found very rich men to support him. The theatre is not as commercial in Germany, or wasn't, as it is here. Theatres were either subsidised by cities, by countries, by governments or rich people put up money.

Reinhardt always found many rich people to put up the money for him. One wealthy man who had made a fortune during the First World War—his name was Camillo Castiglioni—and Reinhardt bought with his money a very old theatre, it was about 180 years old, it's that much older now, and he spent a lot of money (he was always a great artist at spending money) having the theatre renovated. He didn't have it re-built because it had magic acoustics. Wherever you sat, no matter how low the actor spoke you could understand him. He took the wallpaper, which was old and torn, and had the same pattern woven of silk in Belgium, and then covered the theatre with it. He hung in the centre of the theatre a crystal chandelier, which he had made in Venice—it's still there, you can go to Vienna and see it with, I think, four hundred candles. But because the theatre was high with three galleries, he arranged for this chandelier to go up and down. At the start of the performance it was in the middle of the theatre. As it went up, the candle lights faded very slowly. It's really one of the most beautiful theatres in the world. I started in this theatre as an apprentice. There used to be apprentices, I had not yet finished my schooling and it was before I went to university. I still remember my first appearance was at the opening of this theatre, and Reinhardt directed the first four plays. He had all the greatest stars of the German stage assembled, and they all worked for less in this theatre. He called his group the Actors of the Theatre in Der Josefstadt and they all became chartered members. He started with a play by Goldini, *Servant of Two Masters*, and without a set. He had no curtain. The stage became an extension of the auditorium, and was very beautiful. He did the entire play in the baroque style and the scene changes were effected by actors, young actors, who carried out furniture. He had special music written for it. I was one of the actors and my part was to carry on, with other young people, chairs and tables, and at scene changes to carry them off. That was my first acting job. I also played in the park the part of Lysander in *A Midsummer Night's Dream*, but that is always a misunderstanding in my biographies. That was not for Reinhardt—it was done by somebody else, but *A Midsummer Night's Dream* was always connected with him because he did so many productions—among them a film—but somehow it is always said that I did it for him, but it was not true. I stayed in this theatre, played a few more small parts and then became bored and took on a job to go to Prague where there was a German theatre. The manager-director, was only half-a-year with Reinhardt—a man called Leopold Karma who was an actor himself. I remember I played two parts there—one was a role in a German farce called *Frei Frankfurt* which was about the Rothschild family.

Certain things, even while I tell them to you in this conversation, I would not like to have printed because they concern other people's private business, or they are opinions which I offer you privately. As a professional, for instance, I don't think it is my place to talk about other directors, about other films, particularly in a critical way.

People often ask me "Who is your favourite actor, your favourite director?" This is a childish question, and can only have a childish answer; but also I don't think it is professional for me to answer. I'm not a critic but naturally I will have opinions about everything, films and otherwise, but in writing and in public, I don't think it is my place to make these statements. I don't want to say anything bad about another director, particularly a director younger than I am.

After the revolution in Austria, my father, who used to be, as I told you, in the government of the Austrian Empire, was viciously attacked by various political parties and by the newspapers. I remember one day, I was still smaller than nine years, immediately after the First World War, my parents were together at this *Gasthof.* My mother was very unhappy and cried because they said something bad about my father, and my father said—and I learned this from him and I shall never forget it—he said, "If you act in public you must be able to accept public criticism, whether it is right or wrong, whether it is libellous or ill-informed," and he always refused to defend himself. I try to be like him. You will never find a letter from me to a newspaper.

I never forgot my father's advice. But I educated myself very early to be as unaffected as possible by biased criticism. Nobody is completely insensitive to what other people say about him. Like everybody else I prefer people to say good things or write good things about me rather than bad comments. But it has helped me very much, because I really am not as vulnerable as are other directors or actors or people in show business. I don't like bad reviews as well as I would like good ones, but I forget them; I don't worry about them. That is part of my father's heritage. He taught me this, and I remembered the words he spoke to my mother. He felt this, and I believe that if you are acting in public you've got to let people talk about you the way they feel. One result, which maybe comes directly from that, and which at one point or another I should have corrected, is the image of me as a director always shouting at

Preminger with Joan Bennett in his own MARGIN FOR ERROR

every actor all the time. You have been on my sets, you know this is really not true. There might sometimes be a good reason why I am perhaps impatient when people are late, or don't know their lines, or if I find that an actor is in his nature complacent and needs to be shaken up a little. But generally, except in one instance where I fired an actor, I usually part with actors very good friends. Ask them about me and you will find that I am really not as horrible as all these stories make me out to be. They probably come from the fact that I played some Nazis! [Preminger was the Commandant in Billy Wilder's *Stalag 17* and played a Nazi in his own *Margin for Error*.]

In Vienna we lived first in one apartment and I still remember the address, the Eighth—I don't know how you say it in English—*Arrondissement*. It's like a district. In a big city like New York there is only Manhattan, Queen's; but basically Manhattan is New York. In Vienna there were twenty-one districts and I lived in the Eighth District first, and then my father moved from there and we lived in the First District, exactly across from the University of Vienna, I forget the exact number! I lived there until I married Marion Mill, and then I had a small apartment built on to an old house—a very modern apartment. I was always very fond of modern furniture, modern things. I lived there until I left for the United States. I had an affectionate relationship with my mother, a wonderful, warm-hearted woman, but she did not really play a large part in the formation of my character. She was very warm, she loved me, when I was sick as a boy she was terribly upset. But intellectually my father influenced me more than my mother. I had one brother—Ingo Preminger—who now, as you know, has produced his first film with tremendous success. He became a lawyer and actually practised law.

I remember only a few incidents in the First World War. My father was drafted into the Army as the Army's General Prosecutor. There were several spy and treason trials, among them the famous trials against Kramars and Beneš (who later became President of Czechoslovakia) and other people. He was sent to Graz, which is a small town in Austria where they had a kind of political concentration camp. He let many people go who were interned there, like everywhere during the wars, because they were of various nationalities. At that time of the Austrian Empire the enemy was Russia and all the Slavs became suspect. While my father sorted this out I went to the school in Graz. And again it is very interesting that you remember certain events from childhood. I couldn't have been more than about eight years old.

In Austria's school system, I am speaking about the old Austria, the Empire, religion and state were not separate like here, or in Canada and in England. As it was a Catholic country, every school had to give instructions in religion. When I went to Graz there were very few Jews there. Graz, like Linz where Hitler was born, was one of the original homes of anti-Semitism. I went to this school and I could not get instruction in the Jewish religion. My fellow students found out that I was Jewish and they waited for me in hiding. They beat me up terribly, I was bleeding. I still remember because this is a very profound thing in a man's life and character—something like this from youth is never forgotten. I was so humiliated that I did not want to tell this to my parents. I went home bleeding and I said "I fell down." I never told them, never, what the cause was, that there was an anti-Semitic attack against me. They never knew about it, it healed and I lived as well as I could with these circumstances. It's strange that a child would not tell his parents because he did not want them to feel guilty, and I try to watch this in my son. Because in Austria my father was in a socially higher position, we did not really suffer from anti-Semitism; but this terrible incident which happened to me in boyhood, apparently left some mark on me. Otherwise I wouldn't remember it so vividly and find it so hard to forget. But it teaches you perhaps to be more tolerant than you might otherwise be. Certainly as far as I know, as far as I am aware (you can never tell), I have no prejudices. I mean not only racial prejudice, but any social prejudice against people. I hope I am not a social snob of any kind. I have no feelings that people are poor or maybe not successful or are lesser people. Whether I would have been this way in life or not without this incident, I don't know. I tried to protect my parents. I did not let them know that this had happened because I was afraid. I don't know what I was afraid of, but I was ashamed, and apparently ashamed for them. At that time most Jews in Austria were assimilated. There was some anti-Semitism. My father was the first and only Prosecutor, General Prosecutor, who was Jewish, and at one time he was told before he got the job that he should perhaps convert. He was brought up to be more religious than I am, and he said "No, I won't become Catholic just to get this job."

Years later, after I had taken over the theatre from Reinhardt, I was asked to become the head of the State Theatre in Vienna, and a contract was worked out for seven years. It was a tremendous honour for a young man. You must realise that we here live in a very youth-oriented country, and in a youth-oriented society, but at that time, at my age, it was something like twenty-six, to be offered the job of running the State Theatre, the oldest theatre with the greatest tradition maybe in all of Germany, was unbelievable. When the contract was ready, I was asked to come to the Minister's office, the Minister for Education, and I still remember the room. It was a huge room in old baroque, and in one corner a Catholic altar where Catholics kneel and pray with a picture of a saint over it. This is hard to believe, for Austria was already a democracy and a republic, still there were many left-overs like this office, from the old times. To meet the Minister was a tremendous honour and he said to me: "Mr. Preminger, we are very happy to have you under contract, and I would very much like personally to be your (I don't know how you say it—like the best-man at a wedding) witness when you convert to Catholicism." I said to him: "But I have no intention to be baptised." He replied "It was only a minor formality, we never had a man running the theatre who was not Catholic, and it's just a formality." So I said "If it is a form-ality then I certainly don't have to do it." At that, he very politely said good-bye, and my contract was torn up.

At that point, and I must make this clear, I never went to any reli-gious prayers, or services or any church, nor prayed; but it was this experience in my early youth, when I was beaten up because I was Jewish, and denied the job at the State Theatre, which made me feel more Jewish than I would have been otherwise. And if I had agreed to "convert" at that time I would not have been able to accept the offer from Joseph Schenck, which came about a year later, and I would have been in Vienna when Hitler arrived and, as you know, for Hitler there was no baptism. Anybody who was born, or even in any way related to Jews, was a Jew, and I might, like many of my friends, have been killed in a concentration camp, and not gone to America. The fact that I came to America also made it possible for me to have my family come out.

I left Vienna three years before Hitler came. By that time I had become very successful in the theatre. I gave up acting when I was about nineteen and I had started to direct in a theatre in Aussig, which is now in Czechoslovakia. Then I came back to Vienna and I started a theatre on my own, together with another actor who was married to an actress who was in private life a countess and had lots of money. That theatre still exists. It's called The Komedia—The Comedy. I left after two years, I think, and started (with another actor) a theatre in a huge building, a popular theatre, with very low prices, and this lasted for one year and then I went back to Reinhardt as a director. Reinhardt had hired me for the Josefstadt Theatre and after a few years, I think two or three, he decided to retire as practical man. The theatre had lost a lot of money—I took over with the help of this very rich man I mentioned, Castiglioni, and made the theatre a paying proposition. Reinhardt came only once a year to direct the players.

One day a man from America came to Vienna called Joseph M. Schenck, who was the head of 20th. Century-Fox. He had just merged a small company—20th. Century—with Fox, and he needed young people. He said he had heard about me and invited me to his hotel. He said "I hear you are a very good director. Any time you want to come to America, just write to me." I didn't take it too seriously until they told me who he was and that he meant it. It was a very old dream of mine, and nothing to do with Hitler, to go to America. It is maybe difficult to understand when you are here, but there was a romantic idea in Europe about the New World, the possibilities in the New World. When I found that Schenck was serious, I immediately went to Reinhardt and told him I would have to leave as soon as possible and to appoint somebody else for the job of managing director of the theatre, which he did. I directed three more plays, stayed six more months, and started to learn English, and on October 16, 1935, I left Vienna—somewhere I have a photograph that was taken. My wife came later. I went to New York first because I had an appointment on the *Normandie* with Gilbert Miller. Gilbert

Miller was a producer, an American who lived most of the time in England, and looked down on America. He came very often to Vienna, he saw productions that I did and we were quite friendly. When he heard that I was going to America to 20th. Century-Fox he was very economy-minded. He figured he could save a trip, because Fox paid for it (I had written to Joe Schenck and he said, "Fine, just call our representative and they will give you the tickets and everything") and get me to direct *Libel*, an English play which I had directed in Vienna, and also translated after I had taken English lessons. Edward Wooll was the author. Miller asked me to direct it in New York, so I stopped over here and started to rehearse immediately. It opened—I remember it because it was the day after my birthday—on December 6, 1935. I forget whether it opened in Philadelphia then, or New York, I think Philadelphia. And then two weeks later New York, and then on January 2, 1936, I went to Hollywood.

My parents left Vienna the day Hitler arrived—it was March 11, 1938, before Czechoslovakia. It was my mother's birthday and she and my father boarded a train and went to the border. My brother escaped to Czechoslovakia, which was still safe. My parents were stopped at the border, the guards knew my father's name, and sent him back to Vienna. I remember I was in Hollywood, and I was all night on the phone, trying to reach certain friends who I thought had influence, friends of my father in Berlin, but I couldn't reach them. But my father had a friend who was the President of the Police in

Vienna, and he put him on a plane and let him escape to Switzerland. And that's how he was saved. Then from Switzerland he came here and I used certain influences, one of them was Tallulah Bankhead, who behaved beautifully, to make them American citizens. They came on a visitor's visa and the quota for immigrants was filled. Tallulah's father and her uncle were Senator and Speaker of the House respectively. She was a friend of mine. When she heard that my family would have had to leave the country again, she talked to her father and her uncle and they brought in a special Bill for my family to become citizens. She did this without telling me. Only after it was brought in did she call me, I went to Washington and met her father and her uncle. I was always grateful, she was a wonderful woman.

I never was particularly fond of Vienna. I always liked Berlin better. Berlin was a much more exciting city. It was very international, and therefore with much less prejudice. I had a very good friend and actor there, called Conrad Veidt. I was already a director and I used to go to Berlin at least twice a month and we had a wonderful time there. Berlin before the Second World War—between the two World Wars—when I started to travel, was very exciting. What people *think* Paris was, Berlin *really* was. You could get up at five in the morning and go out and find twenty night clubs open, of many kinds. At the hotel I stayed in, the Eden Hotel, women were always beautifully dressed, and there was tremendous energy in Berlin. Vienna to me was always a kind of provincial town. Vienna has a certain beauty, but I think the people are hypocritical: they speak of a love for music and the dance, and they are very polite. I must say when I went back to Vienna to do *The Cardinal*, except for one experience (again with the Minister of Education—another Minister of Education!), they were very polite and gave me a medal. On my sixtieth birthday I got a letter—which I didn't even answer—from the Mayor of Vienna, and they gave me an honorary scroll. But for me, while I am not vindictive, and while I don't think that we can make the people who live now responsible for what happened, the very fact that many of my friends whom I still remember, many people who were wonderful people, were killed there senselessly, is difficult for me to forget. I like to stay away from there. It is not a question that I want to take revenge. When I went there I worked and talked to everybody, even to the actors whom I knew behaved badly, as Nazis and under the Nazi *régime*. I felt that they were punished enough. But frankly if I had to, or would choose to live outside the United States, I could imagine very well living in London, or anywhere in England; and I could imagine living in France and Switzerland. I couldn't imagine going back and living in Vienna. I would feel I betrayed the memory of these people who lived there and died there, by living there now. It's hard to say, it is probably unfair to Vienna. I believe that Vienna is more beautiful for tourists, for people who go there for a couple of weeks and see the sights, Vienna Woods and the Opera, the theatre that I described to you; but when you know the language and you know the people then I cannot get rid of a feeling that these people even today would be capable of starting the whole thing again; but I don't feel this way about Berlin—the northern part of Germany. But in Vienna and Bavaria, where Hitler's home was, it might take generations to completely get rid of it.

While I was running the theatre in Vienna, I made a small film called *The Great Love*, a film I would rather forget! But the Cinémathèque Française unearthed it somehow and has played it. I didn't see it. As a matter of fact, I am tempted to ask them to send me a copy so that I can see it sometime. One of the actors, one of the leads, is still a very big star in Vienna, called Attila Hörbiger, and he was also a tremendous Nazi during the last war, so much so that his own brother who was also a star, didn't talk to him. And he is married to an actress, Paula Wessely, whom I discovered, perhaps not discovered, but I gave her her first serious part. She played only comedy until she came to my theatre. Her first serious part as I remember was in an American play, it was *Front Page*. She is still one of the greatest stars. As a matter of fact she has also some daughters acting. After the war she felt so guilty about having become, maybe more than necessary, a Nazi, that she tried to kill her daughters with a kitchen knife and she was interned for several years. But she was cured and she and her husband are perhaps the biggest stars in the State Theatre I told you about. I saw them when we were in Vienna. We didn't discuss all these things. *The Great Love* was a comedy. The other lead role was played by Hansi Niese, a very famous Viennese elderly comedy star, like an Ethel Merman type. She played the mother and the young man played the son. All I remember is that it was called *The Great Love*, which meant the mother's love for her son, and he at one point

—this actor was very athletic—jumped into the Danube. It was one of the action scenes. The film was financed by a man who owned some movie theatres and was very rich. He also had an interest in the studios in Vienna. As I was very successful in the theatre he offered to finance the picture, but for the matter of money it was, of course, not very much. I made the film and it was quite successful. I remember it opened in the biggest Vienna theatre, "The Emperor," but I don't remember the actual circumstances or what the reviews were.

I have one thing I would like to explain. Part of my make-up or character, perhaps part of my self-education is that I don't collect any old reviews, scrapbooks, anything. I always try to finish whatever I have to do and go on to something new. This is perhaps an almost neurotic fear of being caught up in the past. I feel that in order to be able to work I need to forget what I have done. For instance, when the film is finished, like right at this moment Junie Moon, *while I still went on Saturday to this preview in Boston, I assure you I couldn't watch or listen. I was interested in the reaction of the people and I talked to them at the end. But I am not capable of analysing myself or my work, or remembering things. I remember the films I have made, but not always in the order in which I have made them. I had some legal problems today about films made within the last few years, and I really forgot whether I made* Anatomy of a Murder *first and* Exodus *after, or the other way around, or when* Advise and Consent *was made, and these are comparatively recent pictures. I always tell the story about some of the pictures I really forget. I saw in Paris recently a picture called* Angel Face *(because my wife wanted to see this at the Cinémathèque Française) but I really had forgotten most of it. When I saw it, it all came back, but because it is past, I don't remember how I did it. I have a good memory for things I want to remember, I remember faces I want to remember, if I feel these people mean something to me. Names are difficult, but faces I usually remember. I just don't know why, I want to go on to something new.*

I must tell you that when I arrived in New York I was absolutely overwhelmed. I arrived here on October 21, 1935; it was a beautiful day—they call it Indian Summer, as you know. I came by ship and when I saw, as in a movie, the skyline of New York coming closer and the Statue of Liberty, it may sound sentimental, but it is an unforgettable experience. I must say the remarkable thing about New York and America then was a very real warmth and hospitality. I didn't speak English very well, I had only taken lessons for twelve months, as a matter of fact, when I directed this play I talked about. It was lucky that I had translated it from English into German and knew the play by heart, or otherwise I didn't know what the actors were saying to me; particularly as it was an all-English cast. I was invited out practically every evening; I was impressed. In most other countries where you don't speak the language well, people either make fun of you or ignore you. But here they all tried to help, they felt that you liked America. After I was invited to dinner, I used to go to all-night movies on Forty-second Street and sit through the same film several times, through the night, to improve my English. I still love New York, more than any city in the world. People often ask me: "How can you live here, this nightmare." I don't find it this way, I find it warm, hospitable; I like to talk to taxi-drivers, I don't find people rude as most people do. That's why I moved as soon as I could. I moved back from California to New York, and I feel really at home here.

Gilbert Miller, as I said, I met on the *Normandie*, and on arriving here, I went to work on *Libel*. There was also a man I met, who became my friend until his death, a Roumanian, Felix Fefe. He came here with Miller in the same company. He was a kind of impresario and later on he had a night club here in New York, called "The Monte Carlo." Later he became an agent, a charming man, "Feffay" everybody called him. Miller gave many parties for me. His father-in-law was a very rich man, called Jules Bache, who had a beautiful house on Fifth Avenue. On January 2, 1936, I went to California by myself, and about the middle of January my first wife followed me from

Vienna and joined me there. I remember the journey was long and I was very much impressed by the train, the fact that there was a shower was new for me! Los Angeles seemed very glamorous. They had a big suite for me in the Beverly Hotel. This was at the height of the star system, and Joseph Schenck gave a big party for me, not only with the stars, even Thalberg was there. He was a legendary character, as you know. During the years I was in Vienna working in the theatre, I saw films like other people but I didn't know much, and only certain stars like Clark Gable, Garbo, Chaplin, who I knew because I saw their films. I remember meeting Chaplin several times when I was in California. I didn't know him very well. At that time there were many parties, and it was at Mary Pickford's house where I met Chaplin. I met practically everybody this way, not necessarily intimately.

I didn't stay too long in California, in this first, more glamorous, period. At first, I observed picture making for about eight months at the Fox studios. Then Zanuck called me in and said: "Are you ready to make a film?" and I said "Yes." Then he said, "I have this son-of-a-bitch here who made one film and I pay him a fortune and I don't want to lose more money on him." The son-of-a-bitch was a man called Lawrence Tibbett, the famous singer, and I made a film with him costing less than his salary, and we had a wonderful time in spite of his differences with Zanuck. It was a small film called *Under Your Spell*, and it was not at all bad. Actually, it was a B picture. This was not because Zanuck was mad at me, he wanted to give me a chance, he was mad at Tibbett. He had a contract for two pictures, and he got something like $100,000 per film. The first film was called *Metropolitan*—it was a flop! Zanuck wanted to settle this contract with him and Tibbett said: "No, I want my whole twelve months." So Zanuck said to me: "You can practise on the son-of-a-bitch . . ." At that time the B picture producer was an executive called Sol Wurtzel. His associate producer was called John Stone (and now I owe to John Stone my actor, Ken Howard, who was in my last picture). Wurtzel would take his shoes off at story conferences; but he never read anything.

Lawrence Tibbett and Arthur Treacher in UNDER YOUR SPELL

He had two writers with him, one was a woman, and they came and read to him. His radio was always going, which drove me crazy. He loved football, or baseball, or whatever it was—and when the baseball game came on he turned it up louder and interrupted the story conference.

John Stone was not the producer but he was a very nice man. This was the production team for *Under Your Spell*. I can talk about John Stone and Ken Howard. John Stone, by the way, died a very rich man. Although he never made more than $750 or $1,000 a week, he invested in real estate, and made a fortune. I had a friend, a Hungarian, an agent called George Marton. He came to my house for lunch one day and met Mrs. Stone. Four weeks later I asked Marton again for lunch and he said: "I can't come, I'm playing tennis with Mrs. Stone." I was kidding him about this, and he said: "Don't kid me, if she gets a divorce, I'm going to marry her." And he did. Years and years go by and John Stone died in the meantime and left his son, a writer. About a year ago I got a call from him, and he said, "I am opening our musical and George (meaning George Marton) and my mother are coming from Europe, will you also come?" I went to *1776*, saw Ken Howard and hired him to play the lead in *Junie Moon*! This is all very far-fetched, but I want to show you how life takes strange turns involving people one has known over the years. For instance, there was a song in *Under Your Spell*, where they went on a little mule wagon. From time to time when I am on television on the Merv Griffin show, I see there my friend, Arthur Treacher, who played in the film. He is a charming man.

As the years go by, sometimes we don't see actors and well-known people for a long time, sometimes we meet them again. You're younger than I am and as life goes on we meet many people we remember. There are certain things in a man's life which are memorable. I had an argument on radio a few nights ago. I was on the Barry Gray Show with a young man who writes for the National Review, which is a very reactionary paper. He said that Franklin D. Roosevelt was a dreadful President, and I disagreed. One of my really great experiences was when I directed a play in 1938 with Laurette Taylor
—Outward Bound—*and Mrs. Roosevelt selected this play to go to Washington on Roosevelt's Birthday. He came to see it, and after the play we were at the White House, and I sat next to him. I met him, and it is difficult to explain that for somebody who came here from Europe, he really was a hero. I had read all about him. His personality was exceptional. There is only one other political person who impressed me, like this, although I have met many Presidents (I met Truman, I knew John Kennedy for twenty years, and he gave a luncheon for me at the White House), but Franklin D.*

Roosevelt and Nehru are the two who I shall never forget because of their personalities. I am very rarely impressed, but they both had qualities very similar. They conveyed the feeling when talking to them that they really cared. Maybe this is just a politician's art, but I felt at that moment that these very busy people had nothing on their minds but the person they were speaking to. They were briefed, they knew everything about me, and it was remarkable.

I met Nehru when I was working on a picture of Gandhi and I went to India to do research. It was to be called The Wheel, but I never made it. To read in the papers what Nehru was doing, it wouldn't seem likely he had a minute to spare. I waited three weeks, and when I finally saw him he kept me for two hours. It was a wonderful experience. The reason I didn't make the picture is because the more I knew about India, the more I felt that this should really be filmed with an Indian actor and by Indians. Because, even as we read about him, we cannot understand. Their reactions are different from ours. No actor, in my opinion, no Occidental actor, can really portray Gandhi's multi-faceted character. He was a very down-to-earth man, he hated to be called a saint, yet by our standards he was kind of a saint. Here was a man, for instance, who was not a religious fanatic, but he and his wife at the age of thirty-two after they had, I don't remember, one or two children, said we have done our duty, no more sex. And he gave up sex for life. This gesture was taken without the bonds of religious vows. He was a very practical man. I felt that physically and emotionally, it's very difficult for us to understand their life and it would almost be like trespassing into an unknown area. I think it belongs to them—not to us.

My second film was made at a time of crisis because Zanuck had discovered a French actress called Simone Simon, and he cast her in a comedy. At that time there was a fashion, a trend, for very fast-speaking comedies. I told him: "She won't be able to talk, I can't talk like this." He said: "She'll do it," but she couldn't so he dismissed her and put Ann Sothern in her place. I made a film with her, called

Danger, Love at Work, and Zanuck was enchanted with my work. He wrote to his friends about me, and he invited me to his house. It is very difficult for you, or for anybody today to visualise the power of that man. Zanuck is today Chairman of the Board of 20th. Century-Fox, but there is no comparison to what it meant then. This was really an autocratic system. There were six or seven studios with the head of every one being a dictator. The stars were the only people they had to cater to.

I had a friend, a charming man, a Russian actor named Gregory Ratoff, who was Zanuck's friend, everybody's friend, and my friend. He came to me and he said: "You are going to get the biggest assignment at the studio." Shortly I received a script called *Kidnapped*,

Ann Sothern, Jack Haley, and Edward Everett Horton in DANGER, LOVE AT WORK

based on the story by Stevenson. I considered myself a literate man but I hadn't even heard in Vienna about the writer or his book. The whole idea of Scotland, the Highlands, was something foreign to me —except I knew the Scots wore kilts. Even my English at that time was not far enough advanced for me to be able to read the book. I read the script and the next day Ratoff called me and said: "Well, what do you say?" I said: "Gregory, I am going to turn this down because I don't understand it. First of all, I don't have any feeling for horses or things like this, it is just very strange to me." He said: "This is Zanuck's biggest picture." (I remember it had a budget of $750,000 which at that time was fabulous, and he had in it Warner Baxter and Freddie Bartholomew, I think, one of the child actors; and a red-haired girl, I wonder whatever happened to her? She was a new star.) He continued: "If you turn it down they won't talk to you. You just have to do it." He persuaded me, and I started to cast and to direct *Kidnapped*. Zanuck was not in Hollywood, he was in New York for some stockholders' meeting, and when he came back he didn't like what I had done, and I don't blame him. I think it wasn't very good. We got into a fight about a scene with a dog. I don't remember the details any more, but I know that Zanuck claimed there was a scene in the script which I said wasn't in the script, and we got into a tremendous shouting match. I was right, it wasn't in the script. But he got so mad that he threw me out and assigned another director. I had a contract by this time. When I originally came, I was only on an expense visit, but then when I made the first picture and it was successful, I got a very good contract—comparatively. There were about ten more months to run to the option at this point, the first option had to be taken up. I wanted to settle the contract, but I wanted to see Schenck. I must tell you about my relationship with Schenck. He had told me: "I have no son. Any time you want to come to my house, you don't have to call, come. If it's dinner, there will be another plate for you. If it's lunch, there will be another plate. If it's night, another bed for you." He lived like this, he was a very generous man, lots of money and very charming. I called him after this, and I couldn't get him on the phone. It made me mad. There is a difference in certain things between Europeans and Americans. Maybe now I would understand it better, but I felt terrible.

You must also realise that at that time the political situation in Europe had become worse, and I don't remember now what time it was, whether my parents were already here, and I wanted to see him. Zanuck's assistant, Schreiber, called and said: "If you want to settle your contract . . ." and I said "I've got to first see Mr. Schenck." And I would call every morning and his secretary, who was a very charming woman, I forget her name, would say "At the moment Mr. Schenck is very busy, he will call you back." Some excuse. I still couldn't get him on the phone and I became even more angry. I decided that I would not settle my contract, and they did some very ugly little things. For instance, I came to the office one day at the studio and had no office any more. They had closed it and fired my secretary. So I stayed home. Finally Mr. Schreiber requested to see me. He said: "You are breaking your contract, you won't come to the studio." I said: "Why should I come, I have no place to come—if you have work for me, I come." I decided I would use these ten months, I wanted to go back to New York. First I wanted to get a job, but I found out, by talking to people, that the power of Zanuck was so great nobody would give me a job; even friends. I had met a man who was the head of Paramount Studios at that time, called Buddy De Silva, a song-writer. We had a very good mutual friend, an agent called Louis Sherr. I told this agent: "Go to Buddy and ask him if I can get a job, I will do anything." He said: "He won't give you a job because you had a fight with Zanuck. Nobody will give you a job." And they didn't. So I said to myself, "These ten months I will get the money, which was little enough, save it, and finish learning English."

I enrolled in a course (I was interested in life in America) and I went to U.C.L.A. for a course in dramatics! It's funny, because I wouldn't particularly think I would remember the name, there was an actor, a character actor, Anthony Moore (he used to work at Metro) who ran this course in drama. I wrote and I didn't give my real name. I just wanted to watch, not participate. However, he found out who I was, and he threw me out because he thought I was spying. I learned English and about life at the University, because I had nothing to do but to learn. My wife and I were still invited out socially, and then I went to New York and started to establish myself as a stage director. As I couldn't make films I would work in the theatre. I directed several plays, some successful, some not, between 1938 and 1941. I went into partnership with a firm called Aldrich and Myers. I don't remember now the order of events. I know that I did a play with Jack Barrymore called *My Dear Children*, which was very successful. One of the first plays I did was a revival of *Outward Bound* with Laurette Taylor, who was a wonderful actress. In between I was completely broke, as people are if they work only in the theatre.

I remember a very funny incident. My wife and I stayed at the St. Regis Hotel, and after some time I couldn't pay the bill. The manager was Prince Olensky. We were friendly, and he called me one day and said: "Can I see you?" I met him and he said: "The hotel is not crowded and you can stay here as long as you want without paying the bill, but please don't order room service!" So when I wanted a cup of coffee I had to go out! Anyway, I later paid all his bills. [Preminger also directed, for the stage, *Beverly Hills*, *Cue for Passion*, *The More the Merrier* and *In Time to Come* during this period.]

And I directed *Margin for Error* by Claire Booth Luce, which opened on November 3, 1939. I remember the date because a German actor called Rudolf Forster was to play a German count—he was a great star in Germany. (Much later he played a small part in *The Cardinal*.) One day I came to rehearsals and he wasn't there. In the middle of rehearsals, just a week before we were to open out-of-town, he had left, writing a very funny note for me: "Dear Otto, I am leaving to rejoin Adolf (meaning Hitler). Love, Rudolf." It was in German—it sounds much funnier in German! So he went back to Germany. We couldn't find anybody to play the part, so Claire Booth

Luce suggested that I play it. She had watched me when I rehearsed the actors and she said I could very well play a Nazi. I did the part, first reluctantly, on condition that if we didn't get good reviews in Washington I will drop out. But I got very good reviews and continued playing the part. That was the beginning of my second career as an actor. I played this role for ten-eleven months and it was a very big success.

At 20th. Century-Fox, Zanuck at the moment was not present because he had gone to the Army as a colonel, and Bill Goetz, who was his assistant at that time, was running the studio. A producer and writer called Nunnally Johnson had written a very good script called *The Pied Piper* with the man with the beard, Monty Woolley, and Anne Baxter and he wanted me to play a German Nazi officer in it— he had seen me on the stage. I agreed and went there, to the same studio, as an actor. This was 1942. One day my agent called me. I was a client of the Charles Feldman Agency, and a man called Ned Marin represented me there—a very nice man with white hair. He came to me and said he had a great part: "Fox wants you to play your role in *Margin for Error* on the screen." They had bought the picture rights. I said: "I won't do it unless I can also direct it." He said: "You know very well that in this town nobody is going to let you direct it." Imagine, almost seven years had passed since *Kidnapped* yet they still remembered! He talked to them and came back and said: "No, they won't let you direct it, but they are going to pay you . . ." (which for that time was a tremendous amount of money, I've forgotten how much, something like $75,000—staggering!). He said: "You do it— it takes ten weeks, you get your money and go back and direct your plays in New York." I said: "I won't do it." I was terribly annoyed because I felt I was a director. I didn't want all my life to be limited to the stage. I had experienced motion pictures, and I felt terribly upset about this quiet black-listing, because it was no black-list, but it was just that nobody dared annoy Zanuck.

I went away for the weekend, and I was staying with a rather vacuous girl. We had nothing to discuss, and I said to myself, really I

MARGIN FOR ERROR: Preminger with Milton Berle (standing, left) and Joan Bennett

must do something about the situation at Fox. I came back from the weekend on the Monday morning and I called Bill Goetz's office and said I would like to talk to Mr. Goetz. His secretary said, "He's not here, he will call you back." He called me back at eleven o'clock, and I still remember this clearly today. I went into his office and said: "Bill, you want me to play the part in *Margin for Error*." He said: "Yes, I hear you were great and the producer wants you." I said: "But I'm not an actor, I'm a director and I will only do it if you also let me direct, as I directed the play and played in it." I then said: "Don't say anything. I will do it for free, and you pay me only as an actor. I give you my word of honour that if I direct the picture and after a week you think my work is not good, I will continue acting the part, you can assign another director, and I will act like an actor should act—I mean, not be the cause of any trouble. All you can lose is a week's work." He said: "I'll think it over." I called the answering service every ten minutes and finally there was a message to call him. I did, and he said: "It's a deal!" And this is how I got back into directing again.

I had promised this without reading the script, and it was awful. The producer was a nice man called Ralph Dietrich, but he was really not a great producer and I don't think he did much later, or before; also he did not understand this comedy between the Jewish policeman and the German counsel. I was the director and I didn't dare to ask for a re-write because I was on very shaky ground. So, with my own money, I hired a writer to help me re-write the script secretly. He was a man who later became a very well-known director called Samuel Fuller. He was at that time in Hollywood on leave, he was in the Army. I remember in uniform he used to come—I had a little apartment on El Camino Drive, the house still is there—and I remember seeing him from the window arriving in his car carrying a huge typewriter. I didn't pay him much; he came up and we worked on the dialogue, the script, together, and I started the film. After a week's work, Bill Goetz called my agent and asked me to his office. I thought he was going to fire me. Instead he said he loved the rushes and he wanted to sign a contract. But now I felt it was very difficult for a director to get along if he didn't produce his films. He offered me a contract as producer, director and actor. This contract, with certain changes, was the contract I worked (except that I always got more and more money) until I left Fox to become an independent producer. So, when a picture was over I got an assignment, like every producer, and the first picture under this contract was *In the Meantime Darling*, which I produced and directed. But this success, or victory, was short-lived. Zanuck now came back from the army and I have already told you about the meeting at his home (*p.* 8), when he said that as long as he was at the studio I would never direct again, only produce) Now again, I was in the same position as I was several years before, and, on my new contract, with about ten months to go still. There was nothing much going on, it was summer in New York, so I decided I would stick it out. Zanuck, in order to humiliate me, first relegated me to B pictures under Brian Foy.

* * *

IN THE MEANTIME DARLING, with Jeanne Crain at left

I took one story nobody else wanted called *Laura* and another called *Army Wives*. We worked on the script of *Laura* first with Jay Dratler. He was a poet—just yesterday I mentioned his name somewhere. It was delivered to Brian Foy, and he called me in and he said: "David (who was his assistant), David Stevens, read your script and I must say it's no good." So I said: "Brian, don't you think you should read the script? I think it's very good." Using the only way I knew to persuade him, I said: "Brian, David makes about $75 a week. I get $1,500 a week. I like the script, don't you think you should give me the benefit of the doubt and read it?" He said: "Fine!" The next day or the day after, I went up in the elevator to my office and in the elevator was also Brian Foy. "Come with me," he said, "David was right. It's a lousy script." So I said: "Brian, why don't you let Zanuck read the script?" He said: "You know how Zanuck feels about you. Even now he would like to get rid of you. If he reads the script, you'll be out. Work on the other script, on *Army Wives*." (He was the Executive Producer for all my films.) So I said: "No, I want him to read it." He said: "Well, it's suicide, but if you want it . . ." So now I waited and about two or three days later—Zanuck was an incredibly organised man, I don't know how he is now, but he was remarkable then— he called us into this huge office. He always walked up and down with a polo mallet in his hand, and a long cigar. He said to Brian: "Well, what do you think we should do with this?" Brian explained to Zanuck why he didn't like the script. I still remember, Zanuck let him hang himself, he never interrupted him. He said, "This is after all about police officers and not one scene plays at the police station." (We worked on that because naturally that was the whole idea.)

When Brian finished, Zanuck said: "I like the script. I have taken it home." And I was triumphant! Now came weeks which I will never forget. The casting of this picture, and to find a director. Whoever we sent the script to didn't like it. A man who did a lot of musicals called Walter Lang turned it down. Milestone, who was a good friend of mine, turned it down. He told me he didn't like it. He said to Zanuck: "Why don't you let Preminger direct it?" Because he wanted to help. As this happened, one director after another refusing it, Zanuck became insecure. He almost dropped it, when Rouben Mamoulian accepted it. But he later also abandoned it, saying he didn't like the script. But he felt he needed the money, he wanted the money. He got something like $60,000 for direction. And Zanuck hired him. From the moment he got the script, he treated me—I mean the contract—like dirt. Whatever I said he didn't listen to me. He got together with the costume designer and planned different costumes from those I wanted, although Zanuck still worked with me, because he believed in this bureaucracy—the producer/director —and we cast. It came to the question of the part Clifton Webb played. Zanuck and Mamoulian wanted a man called Laird Cregar, who at that time played all the heavies. I, who had worked very hard on the script, felt that the only possibility to make this a success was if people did not know from the beginning that this amusing and very urbane and civil character was the villain. The same friend, Felix Fefe, who knew everyone, knew Clifton Webb, who at that time was playing in Noël Coward's play *Blithe Spirit* downtown in Los Angeles. Felix invited me to come there with some other people, and I was fascinated by Clifton Webb. I had never seen him, or knew who he was, and we met and I felt he must play this part. I told him so, and I gave him a script. He loved it and wanted to play the role. I went to Zanuck very excited. By that time we were quite friendly as a result of working together. He just didn't want me to direct. I went to Zanuck about Clifton Webb, and we called in the casting director, a man called Rufus LeMaire. He was against it. What happened in these studios was that these people always guessed what the executives wanted. They knew. They were trained to know who Zanuck favoured. And Rufus LeMaire felt immediately that Zanuck would not like Clifton Webb. So he said: "You can't have Clifton Webb play this part. He flies." I said: "What do you mean?" I didn't even understand what he meant. I already knew that Clifton Webb was a little effeminate, but that didn't bother me at all. I said I would like to make a test with him. Rufus LeMaire said "Why make a test?

56

Clifton Webb was two years at Metro at a very high salary, and he made a test. I'll get you the test." So I said: "Fine." And he was supposed to get the test. One day, two days, three days, a week, ten days—no test. They always said tomorrow, tomorrow. Fortunately, I met Clifton Webb again at a party, and I said "We are waiting for your test." He said: "What test, dear boy?" I said that Rufus LeMaire, who was casting director at Metro, and who is now at Fox, said you made a test at Metro, and we want to see it. He replied: "My dear boy, I was at Metro for two years or eighteen months, and never faced a camera. Never made a test!" So the next day, at the executive luncheon (there was a long table with Zanuck at the head,

Clifton Webb, Gene Tierney, and (at right) Dana Andrews in LAURA

all producers were permitted to eat there, and from time to time there were guests) I said in front of everybody: "Rufus, when are we going to get the test of Clifton Webb? Is it tomorrow?" and he said "Yes." I said: "You are lying, Rufus, he never made a test." Zanuck was amused by this and said: "What do you mean?" I said: "I talked to him last night and he never faced a camera." LeMaire got very embarrassed. I said to Zanuck: "Now, don't you think it would be fair to let him make a test?" Zanuck said: "O.K., make a test. Call Gene Tierney and make a test and (I don't know where Mamoulian was) you can direct it." Mamoulian was out-of-town, or somewhere.

So I jubilantly drove the same evening down to the Biltmore Theatre, where Webb played, arranged for the test, selected a scene and took it to him, only to hear him say: "My dear boy, I am a star. I don't make any tests. Besides, I know exactly what your friend Zanuck wants to see. If he wants to see me, he can come here and see me in the theatre." So I said: "Clifton, I have fought so much. I got the right to make a test with you and Gene Tierney." And he said: "And who is Gene Tierney?" I described her as a girl who just came from the theatre in New York and made a big hit, and was a big star. He said: "I don't know your Miss Gene Tierney. But because you are so nice, I will make a test for you from a scene in this play." So I went to Zanuck and told him he would rather do a scene from the play, and Zanuck said: "I'm not filming the damn play. I am not interested in the play. I want him to do this from the script."

Now you must realise that it was all crises! Every one of these things. I didn't want Laird Cregar. There was the question of not hurting other people's feelings. I called a test and took a terrific gamble. I couldn't take a scene because I would have had to ask other actors, but in this play is a monologue, a famous monologue. I got a very good cameraman and I photographed Webb in this monologue, without the permission of Zanuck. I knew it was great, and I took the test to Zanuck. He didn't say anything and we screened it. Zanuck looked at me, and being a professional, he liked it. He said: "You son-of-a-bitch, I told you I don't want to see the play, but O.K.," and he let it play. Later on Zanuck and Webb became the greatest of friends, he practically lived in Zanuck's house in Palm Springs. So that was set. Mamoulian was not very happy because he didn't like him when he started the picture, and Zanuck again had to go to New York. We saw the rushes and they were awful! Lou Schreiber, who was Zanuck's assistant, and I was his assistant after Bill Goetz had left, said to me: "You've got to send those rushes to New York," because even he didn't like them.

Then came a wire from Zanuck in New York to Lou Schreiber, who gave it to me. Everything was blamed on me, and Mamoulian was to start the picture again, but without any "interference" from me. In the meantime Mamoulian, who didn't talk to me, who didn't permit me on the set, had also gone to Zanuck. He started again, and it was worse than before. Zanuck came back and looked at the stuff and we had lunch again, and in front of all the people he said to me: "Do you think we should take Mamoulian off the picture?" I said "Yes." He took him off the picture, went back to his office, called me and said: "You can start directing on Monday!" Of course, I was very happy, except that all the actors were against me, because Mamoulian called them all on the set and said, "I want to say goodbye, I am fired, and you will not stay long if Preminger doesn't like your performance." I came to start on Monday and I still remember Judith Anderson changing her costume and saying: "I'm glad you are directing, Mr. Preminger. It's so bad, show me what to do." Being an actor, I played the scene for her. "You do this exactly the way I show it to you. Then I would like you to come tomorrow morning and see the rushes and on the screen you will see the difference." She did, we became friends, everything worked out, and I directed the film. When it was finished, I showed it to Zanuck, the rough cut, as usual. He was surrounded with people, among them a French producer who taught him French. They were trained to see in the back of his neck whether he liked it or not. He didn't like it. The picture was over and he said: "Well, we missed the bus on this one," and left.

That night, I remember it was raining in California, and my poor cutter, Lou Loeffler and I were left standing there, in front of my car in the parking lot. He couldn't understand it. You always know, when you run a film for the first time, the rough cut, if there is something to it. We felt there was. The next day Zanuck called me and said: "You made a chorus girl out of Gene Tierney and we must re-do the last third of the picture." If you remember, the picture has one narration by Clifton Webb and one by Dana Andrews. Now he added a completely new version of what happened, seen from Gene Tierney's point of view. He brought in a writer, and walked up and down and dictated, and at one point he stopped and saw my face and said: "You don't like it?" I said: "No." So he said: "If you don't like it, have somebody else direct it." Anyway, the script was finished by this writer, I forget his name, he later committed suicide (not because of that! He was a studio hack). And I directed this stuff—it was really impossible—about two weeks' re-takes. The actors laughed! I persuaded them to do it. Again the rough cut of the new version was ready, and scheduled for nine p.m. and at lunch in the dining room, there was a guest. This is remarkable and this is why you have to believe in fate, or something. The guest was Walter Winchell, who is a friend of Zanuck. Zanuck said to him: "Walter, tonight I have to work late and then I'm seeing a film at nine. Come and see the film. After the film, we can have supper together."

At 9 o'clock there we were, Zanuck, my cutter and I, and not the yes-men any more who, by the way, had all sent letters with suggestions which were unbelievable—they were so stupid! In the last row of this four-or-five row projection room was Walter Winchell with a girl. For the first time when the picture went on, particularly the dialogue of Clifton Webb, there were laughs from Walter Winchell, giggles from the girl. The picture was over, and Winchell gets up and says to Zanuck (I don't know if you ever met him, he speaks in short sentences) "Darryl, that was big time—big time—Great, great, great! But you are going to change the ending? What's happening at the end? I don't understand." This again is where you can see that Zanuck, who is a flexible and a professional man, instead of being mad like the other people might be, he looked at me and said: "Do you want to have your old ending back?" I said: "Yes, sure." He said: "O.K." I threw everything out, all the re-takes, put the old ending back, we had a preview and it was brilliant. That is the story of how *Laura* became a success, and how I became a director again.

I'll tell you about the music from Laura *by David Raksin, which became very famous. As a director, I don't know much about music. I have only an instinct for music in connection with my films. I am not a music-lover, I have not a very good ear. When I was young in Vienna I used to go to the opera, but I don't go to concerts or the opera any more. This is what happened with* Laura. *Because the film had a very bad reputation at the studio, after the re-takes started, and at the time the musicians were assigned, Alfred Newman, the head of music, and tremendously powerful, decided that he would not waste his time writing the music. He assigned a young man and sent him to me—Raksin. He came to my office and we started to discuss the score. He looked at the rough cut, and I said I needed a theme. He and I suggested that we should buy a tune that I liked very much—Gershwin's* Summertime—*and get the right to use it as the main theme. We couldn't get the rights. One day Raksin came to my office (I had a little piano there) and he said: "Let me play this to you." He played the theme. I said then: "I don't know much about music, as I told you, but I like this, let's put it in." This was before the picture became "rescued" by Winchell. This is the theme* Laura, *and only after the picture was finished and released, did Mercer write the lyrics, which I still don't like. Mercer doesn't like me because I expressed this! When I became an independent producer I devised a new system. As you probably know, usually when a film is finished, the director shows the rough cut to a composer and then he has about four to six weeks to write the score. I feel that this is not enough time, so I assign a composer when I start shooting, or before I start shooting. He is with me on the set, he sees the rushes. If he has suggestions according to the script, like providing him with a little more time in a scene, I listen to him. I was very lucky with this method. With this system, however, I cannot use very successful composers because they are too expensive! A successful composer does several scores a year, and my composer needs to be with the shooting and final editing. When I finish, he has been six months on one score. So I usually have new, young composers. Several times I was very lucky, as with Ernest Gold on* Exodus, *and others. They have time to adjust, to learn about the characters, and sometimes it is better—that is my system.*

Showings for Zanuck were critical times. At that point, as I told you, he cut one-third of the picture out and put a new ending in—here he had the complete power. This was only the rough cut—he had to approve it, he had to approve everything. The danger of this whole system was not that he was not infallible—Zanuck is a very competent man but that he could not always be right. The whole idea of entertainment, and I don't want to sound pretentious and speak about art, is that it is unique, something new, something different, if it is only different in some small way. It is one man's outlook on the world, his interpretation of humanity. Whatever you do—whether it is writing a book or painting a picture—it is one man's work. That is the beauty of it. You cannot make pictures in a factory. This is what happens now in television. I mean, three big companies are trying to manufacture entertainment for all of the United States, and maybe for the world. It doesn't work. It will work less and less, and they will have to come more and more to individualists. The same pattern like the movies. Films were forced to de-centralise, to let individuals concentrate on one film, and give them more freedom, autonomy. The same thing is going to happen in television—it is inevitable. To go back to this factory system: even while it was working, once you had made a success (for instance, after I had made *Laura*) the opposition changed. It was still Zanuck who assigned properties, it was still Zanuck who bought the stories, and I or any other producer could advise him.

I remember one day I was invited to his house in Palm Springs. We had become friends now, and I came out there on Friday and we had dinner, nothing was mentioned. Saturday morning I found myself alone. Suddenly all the other guests were not there, only Zanuck and I, and Charles Feldman, the agent. He was my agent, but he was also the agent of another director. The talk came around to this other director, his name was John Stahl. Zanuck said: "It's very disappointing. I have to stop the making of *Forever Amber*. Something has happened to John Stahl, he is doing a terrible job. So far I have spent two million dollars and now I have to stop it." He turned to me saying: "You will have to continue the film." I said: "Darryl, when the book was submitted to the producers I couldn't even finish reading it, and I told you (we used to write him notes on all the submissions) it was a horrible book. I couldn't make this film." I reminded him that it was just like *Kidnapped*; "If I start it you will fire me." So he said: "Nonsense! You are a member of the team, you now have a contract" (at that time I had a contract for a fabulous weekly sum— I've forgotten how much, I think it was $7,500—it was without options with five more years to run). "You will do this film, you must help me."

It was very difficult. You wanted to get along with him when he talked like this. He said: "I won't blame you. You go in and look at all the material and give me a report on Monday." He had it all set up— the projection room, the cutters, everything. "If you want, you can throw out the whole thing—anything you want." On Monday I saw him and he said: "I hear you didn't like it." I mentioned the little English girl whom they discovered was impossible, and he said: "Go ahead, you do whatever you like." I wanted Lana Turner but he didn't want her because she was at Metro. He wanted Linda Darnell. Anyway, we started on a new script and production. I think it took seventeen weeks, I made the picture and I was unhappy with it. But, oddly enough, I was in Paris and the Cinémathèque Française loved that film! They told me to look at it again, and I will maybe.

FOREVER AMBER : Leo G. Carroll and Linda Darnell

I survived all this because I had
made a success on Broadway. I was
quite well-known for plays and I
could always go back here. Besides, I always had a tremendous
belief in my future. As my wife said
downstairs at dinner, I am an
optimist. I always see the best of
things. When my father had come
to America and I had no job and I
lived at the St. Regis, as I told you,
I couldn't pay my bill. My father

had brought with him some money
which he had saved and kept in
Switzerland. It was not much, and
he suggested that he would buy a
farm, and that the three of us—my
father, brother and myself—would
live modestly in the country, with
this money, and I would give up the
idea of being a director. It was very
tempting, because I was broke, I
had no play, I was out of Hollywood, but I said no. Therefore,

I didn't ask him to lend me money because I was not sure I could pay it back, and I knew this was all he had. Later on, he devoted himself to investing this money and he did fairly well. But at that point it was very difficult. However, I believed —I said "No, I am going to be a director, I'm not going to make any compromises, it will be all right. I don't ask you to give me any of your money, but unfortunately I can't help you at the moment." This is my profession, I believed in it and I worked on. During the period all these setbacks happened —it was not as rational as I am explaining it to you now—not for one moment did I believe that it was the end of me. I always felt that something is going to help me. I believed this was my vocation—it sounds a little over-simplified— but don't think that I did not have,

no, not doubts, but despair some-times when I was low, but I was never without hope. It's part of my make-up. I feel this in many ways. Years later when I was successful, I had overspent. I had a beautiful house in Bel Air, there was a divorce from my first wife, I had a lot of financial obligations, and I hadn't paid my taxes. I was here in New York when my business manager called and said "the Government has attached your house." I said: "Sell it." I never saw it again. Never saw that house, which I loved—like this house, which I decorated—or its paintings and furniture. I never cared because I felt I must be able to detach myself from material things and live. That's the way I feel now. I feel that as long as I can work, to act or direct, I can live.

At the time I got married to Marion Mill, I thought (like everybody else) it was the right thing to do. It was not. My present marriage is my last, and I love my wife very much and the children; this I now know *is* the right thing and I feel very happy. I have no regrets and no bad feelings towards my first two wives, in spite of the fact that in both cases I over-paid for my divorces. When it comes to divorce, women usually get much tougher than men. During this time women have nothing on their mind but the divorce and they feel they want to get everything out of it. Men have their business and their work. I

C

don't mind, the cost of my divorces was worthwhile, because of what I finally found in my last marriage.

Some of my pictures are a success, some are very unsuccessful. I don't worry about it because I feel this is the way a man's life is. We cannot always be successful. Not even the greatest directors. In spite of the fact that he never won an Academy Award, I think Hitchcock is one of the great directors of all times, much greater than many people think, and much more so than some who won Academy Awards. But if you look at his record, he sometimes makes a hit and then three flops. But I admire him, if not some of the pictures he makes. I feel that sooner or later I make one flop then I make a success. I don't worry. I had made a very fast and very spectacular success as a young man in Vienna, and I felt why shouldn't I be successful here eventually, even if there were setbacks? So I have always a great sense of humour and almost I feel a sense of history about it. I remember when Zanuck dismissed me, I felt bad about it; but on the other hand felt that he would be sorry some time! It had to change, and the situation did change completely.

After *Laura* and *Forever Amber* there were no more serious conflicts at Fox. There was, as I said before, an irritation because the whole studio works within the border lines of the tastes and personalities of the studio heads. Agents didn't even submit certain stories to Fox because they felt Zanuck wouldn't be interested. The story department didn't even bother with certain stories because they knew what Zanuck wanted. While we had a choice, we could still assign a story to one or another producer if two or three liked the story submitted, the producers had not the original choice from all the story material available, only from the story material submitted to Fox. I said before, subconsciously a person in this position develops an awareness, knowing, when reading something, without thinking so much about it, that this Zanuck doesn't like so he won't approve it anyway, so why go looking for trouble and conflicts. As I told you before, in the case of *Forever Amber*, I was a member of a team and getting along with Zanuck was sometimes very difficult. It is like having a friend, or being married, working in any other relationship; compromises are made in order to peacefully co-exist. It doesn't necessarily mean compromising to the extent of abandoning one's integrity; but it is not the same thing as going out, as I am doing now, to read a manuscript, or start a book, or hearing about something, or seeing a play, and saying: "I want to do this."

I will do everything in the world as an independent producer to get the financing and distribution, to film this particular story and not consider anyone else. Naturally, I am still limited because I have to get the approval of the people who finance it, and distribute it; except in a few exceptions, like in my last contract with Paramount where I didn't need this approval for two or three films. The "independent" however is never completely without having to account to someone or to talk to somebody about what he wants to do. It depends, also, in this business, on the moment of success. Right after a success it is easier. You are more wanted by the people than if you have just made a less successful picture. All these things are self-explanatory, anyway.

However, the whole development of independent directors-producers is a tremendous step forward in films; and with this step forward we come also to the point where basically the story and the director have become more important than the stars. The star system is gone. That doesn't mean that I would not want Elizabeth Taylor if I felt she is the right actress for the part. She is a very good actress and if she gives a good performance, and if the enterprise and the story are right, she contributes naturally, like any good actress; or maybe a little more because she has a following. So it is also foolish to be blind to the virtues of a star, a prominent actor or actress. In other words, any generalisation is wrong. Every situation, every story, every cast must be judged individually.

*　　　*　　　*

Within the framework of the studio, after the success of *Laura*, I was as independent, as autonomous as any producer, any director, at that time could be. But it was *within* the framework of the studio, in other words, some stories would not even be submitted to me because Zanuck might decide before they were sent to anybody that he wanted to produce them, or he wanted to give them to somebody else. There was a story I wanted to make very much. It was about a racial problem, *Pinky*. I discovered this story and brought it to the studio. Zanuck decided John Ford should direct it. I was very unhappy, and I went to him and he said: "No, I want to produce this myself with John Ford as director." There was nothing else to do. I was too proud to beg for something. John Ford started the story. It didn't work out and he was taken off. Then Kazan took it over. I thought, of course, that I could have done it better, whether it is true or not, who knows. These things are inevitable because Zanuck ran the studio, and he ran it his way, and I as a grown-up person had to recognise this. I had a contract, got paid, and did the things I wanted to do within the limitations they imposed on us. I was always free to say: "I won't do it," and there were many things I turned down at that; but there was never a big conflict as in the beginning, and there were never any more suspensions. I received stories, not scripts. I didn't look for something, I read many, many things. Certain things suddenly catch the attention, for some reason; I am interested, my passions aroused, they make me enthusiastic. It is not something that I can analyse—it is this, or that—and maybe sometimes later I feel I made a mistake and shouldn't have done it.

I have often bought stories even as an independent producer with complete freedom, worked on the script for many months, and then dropped it because my enthusiasm cooled off. It is better not to do it and lose the money paid for the story rather than make a film one no longer believes in. I feel in order to make a film and to meet the daily challenges that actually exist during production, I must be enthusiastic and excited about it otherwise it's all so pallid. Many films are announced and stories bought. Eventually, they are sold again, or dropped. At the studio, this money is charged to the next film. This is only normal. It is the same as if you wanted to write a book about somebody and then decided after having a few interviews, no, I had better not try the book, this man is dull. It must have happened to you. You might tomorrow wake up and say: "Why do I need this Otto Preminger!"

My attitude towards writers is unlike that of other directors. I never ask for screen credit, in spite of the fact that I participate very actively on the writing of the screenplay. It is the director's job, and my job as a director, to direct everything—even the writer, just as I direct actors, and this means working with writers for hours at a time and re-writing scenes. The script has to be completely filtered through my brain and through my emotions if I want to direct it. I cannot direct a script that has just been given to me, and I think this participation on my part is the director's job, as it is to direct the designer and all artists and technicians. In other words, the scenic designer might have some ideas about the sets or the locations, but I am the one who finally decides how they should be if I am to direct the picture. The same is true about the actors—which is the popular idea of a director, that he directs actors. The same is true about the editor. Sometimes I laugh when I read in a review, "brilliantly edited by so-and-so." The editor in a film, as you very well know, is not the same kind of editor as the editor in a book. In a book the editor is really performing a very important function, artistically and intellectually, because he is really editing the work of the writer, even if it is with the writer he is still having something to say. In a film, the editor physically carries out what the director tells him to do. I tell him exactly what scenes to use, and he is an extended arm. Naturally, if he is sensitive then he gets adjusted to me and my work becomes easier. For instance, I had for many years an editor, Lou Loeffler, but unfortunately he cannot work with me any more because of an eye operation. He knew practically in advance which scene I would select if there were two or three scenes printed, and he knew exactly

the way I felt, so it was easy for me.
I just had to say a few words and he
knew. But generally speaking, it is

the director who edits the film and
not the editor.

There is not much else to say about my years at 20th. Century-Fox. *In the Meantime, Darling* was a small story I had acquired before *Laura*; then it stuck with me and I had to do it, a minor film I don't even remember. There were two young people in it, and there was much excitement because for the first time in films, the Code permitted us to show married people sleeping in the same bed. *Royal Scandal* was really prepared for Ernst Lubitsch, whom I admired and loved very much, and who was already sick at that time. He directed later again, but his doctor told him not to direct at this time. He chose me, from all the people available. It was an honour because he was considered one of the great directors. I directed the story from a script by him. Someone said I was quite brave, in a way, because everyone talked about the "Lubitsch Touch." I don't worry about these things. I am not brave. I don't think about it. It is part of my philosophy not to worry about what other people think of me. I wish I could teach my little son this. He just came to me crying that the other boys are much better in baseball than he is. What can you say to a nine year old boy? He will get better! I never played baseball, I was always bad in any physical sporting activity, but I didn't care. It is very difficult to learn, particularly when young like he is, but even later, not to care.

I directed the film my way and if people felt that Lubitsch (though I don't remember, I don't think anybody said it) would have done it better, that is their opinion. However, something strange happened with this picture. I learned something from it. We went to a preview and it was very successful. People roared with laughter; still, when we left, I felt something was wrong. We went back in the car, Lubitsch, Zanuck and I, and they were jubilant. I didn't say anything, and Zanuck turned to me and said: "What's the matter with you? Aren't you happy? We have a big hit!" I said: "Darryl, I feel

Anne Baxter with Tallulah Bankhead in ROYAL SCANDAL (known as CZARINA in Britain)

that people didn't like the picture." He said: "You're crazy!" I said: "No, they laughed, but did you notice how they walked out? I felt somehow a let-down." They both laughed, but it was true. The picture was never a tremendous success and I'll tell you why. This was the borderline situation comedy that Lubitsch was so great at, where he took situations and twisted them. He could make everything funny, but he did it at the expense of character. He never worried about the character, and it was after all, the Empress of Russia, and she didn't always act like the Empress of Russia. In the end there were laughs, but I found then, and have learned since, that the public doesn't accept it. They like the integrity of the character to remain intact. Even if they laugh less. Later, when Lubitsch died, I was asked to complete *That Lady in Ermine*. I really didn't think that the script was interesting, nor was the picture. I finished it —that was it.

*   *   *

I am often asked how much freedom did I have in choosing actors under the Fox system. At that time all the studios had their stars. When there was a part for Dana Andrews, who was under contract to Fox, we used him. At that time many actors were away at war, and it was not easy to find those most suitable to certain roles. We couldn't simply go out and hire another man. You heard me today talk to Sinatra. Actually, when I bought *Where the Dark Streets Go*, I did so because I had Sinatra in mind, and I sent it to him. Now if I had been at Fox, it is more than likely we would have just received a memo the day before (these memos used to go around) which said: "When you film your next story, keep in mind so-and-so, who has no assignment." The studios tried to keep their actors busy. I don't think Dana Andrews ever became a monumental star, but then the misfortune of Fox was, it really never had very big stars. They borrowed Clark Gable once or twice because of the relationship of Bill Goetz, Zanuck's executive assistant, to Louis Mayer who was Bill Goetz's father-in-law, and that is why they had access to Clark Gable and others, which other studios didn't have. But Dana Andrews, during those times of war, was one of the respectable leading men. The only bigger star at Fox was Tyrone Power, and we never worked together although we were very good friends.

In this system, the final decision was with the head of the studio, but besides and beyond this you knew what his opinions were, and what his decisions would be, regarding the use of players, and unless there was really a deep conflict between his wishes and the director's integrity, we didn't engage in arguments. In other words, when I had a story like *Fallen Angel*, Dana Andrews was available and I knew that Zanuck (because I was successful with Dana Andrews in *Laura*, and worked well with him) would have wanted me to use him. So before he asked me I would cast him. There was a give and take which, for the ultimate achievement, is not the best system. The ultimate achievement is not to compromise; the ultimate achievement is to look—not only in motion pictures but in anything in life—for the ideal, the very best solution, and then if it is unattainable, the second best. But living in a community, which the studio basically was, with a number of stars, character actors, writers (and writers were not so critical because you could always get an outside writer) meant choosing between them, and it was also a question of becoming friends. As Dana Andrews worked with me and we became friendly, if I insisted on an outside star, when a story suitable for him was to be filmed, Dana Andrews would have come to me and said: "Otto, what have I done to you? This is a very good part for me, I need a part." They are human. We are not, after all, machines. Living with people means recognising certain human considerations which are not always healthy for the ideal film, or the ideal achievement, but they exist. They exist even within independent production.

I don't knowingly make compromises, but, for instance, when I did *Advise and Consent*, I was very happy to find a part (which could be a "come-back part") for Gene Tierney, because I liked her. I did not say maybe Olivia De Havilland could play this better, or Joan Fontaine—I don't know—I didn't even think. I was glad to ask her. This is a fact which exists in any relationship between people. When I did *The Cardinal*, I was happy to find a part for Maggie McNamara who had also been, like Gene Tierney, very ill for six or seven years with a nervous breakdown; it was a life-saving action for her although she never acted again after that. I could give her a part and make her feel wanted again, and it didn't hurt the film. I wouldn't have done so had it hurt the film. In the studio there was beyond that the question of the judgement and the known tastes of the man who ran the studio. It was his studio, it was an autocracy.

After *Laura* when I turned an actor down, he or she was not forced on me. The one exception was when I took over *Forever Amber*. The studio had cast the leading part. I wanted Lana Turner, so I gave a dinner party and invited her. I put her with Zanuck and told her to talk to him. Because Zanuck had told me: "I will not give this part to her." He felt that whoever played this part would be one of the most important stars in the business, and he said: "Lana Turner is under contract to Metro. Why should I do this for Metro?" There were other considerations like this. "If Linda Darnell dyes her hair blonde, she will be just as good." Now she was not just as good, but she was good enough. The picture, in spite of all the whittling that was done, the censorship difficulties, the cuts that were made for the Catholic Legion of Decency, brought back its money and eventually made a profit. It was started twice and two million dollars were thrown out of the window, at that time a tremendous amount of money! If I had been an independent producer I would never give a part to somebody because I thought she will become a star as a result and I can get options on a contract. That doesn't interest me. If I can get options, then fine; but I will always try to get the best possible person for the part.

You will find that actors and I have a very good rapport, *except for one case, which I mentioned, and I don't like to mention by name. I always parted with actors in a very friendly way; like Gary Cooper, who was a very close friend of mine. Charles Laughton, too; it was one of the greatest experiences to become his friend on his last film. And Laurette Taylor; in the book by her sister, she describes how I saved her. I have a very good understanding with actors. You ask them sometimes. I don't want to say this to defend myself.*

As for *Fallen Angel*, I can't even tell you the story of it. I told you the story about the time I was dressing for dinner and *Fallen Angel* was on television. I watched it and I got quite involved; then my wife finished dressing and I never saw the ending. I still cannot recall the ending! It is an interesting film. I had the same experience in Paris with *Angel Face*. My wife hadn't seen it and I went to the Cinémathèque for twenty minutes, but stayed for the whole picture. It was fascinating and I certainly found many things after twenty years which I would do differently now. The performance of Jean Simmons was very, very good and very up-to-date. She was wonderful in this film. Enthusiasts say to me: "It must be very strange watching one of your films without really remembering you did it." It's the same sensation a writer would have going over old papers and looking at articles. You cannot possibly remember all the reviews you wrote, or the interviews you attended. It is the same with a film-maker.

From *Fallen Angel* I went to *Centennial Summer*, a welcome change, a drama to musical. Again, it was an assignment. It was available and

Dana Andrews, Anne Revere, and Alice Faye in FALLEN ANGEL

I liked to work with Jerome Kern. That was his last score, and he died in New York before the film was released. It is very difficult to discuss these films today in detail, because don't forget during these years I also lived. I was married, I got divorced, I married again, I met people, I read books—one develops and changes, so it is difficult now just thinking of the pictures and not remembering the circumstances of my life, what else I did at that time. Perhaps why I did *Fallen Angel*, why I did *Centennial Summer*, was partly because I was working on some other project that intrigued me.

Today, I would not be capable of spending three or four months on *Centennial Summer*—neither the story or the characters would interest me. That is really a film I wouldn't do today. It was successful and it worked, and at that time it probably served some purpose in my life, and in my career. It's hard to say why, I can't tell you why I did it. That is true of many things. I know very well that *Laura* fascinated me, also *Fallen Angel*. *Angel Face* was an interesting incident. One day Zanuck called me and said: "Howard Hughes would like to borrow you." I knew Howard Hughes, and I said: "Very well." He sent me a script called *Murder Story*, and it was awful. I met with him and we drove around in his little car and he said: "Otto, you must do this for me because this bitch (meaning Jean Simmons) has cut her hair short, and I hate short hair. She was mad, took the scissors, and we had a fight. I have her only for eighteen days during a six week period, eighteen days to work with her. If you don't like the story, get some other writers. Do anything you want." So you see I can't talk about every single film I made. Critics and audiences can look at them and say what they like. I can't. It is not my way to go back into the past and to look at my old pictures and to discuss them; I don't want to say this is torture, because I'm not easily tortured. It is really something I just find a waste of time, and I would much prefer you write about me the way I am now! Not dig into my very dark past!

Jeanne Crain, Cornel Wilde, Walter Brennan, and Constance Bennett in CENTENNIAL SUMMER

Filmography—First Period

DIE GROSSE LIEBE. 1931. *Director:* Otto Preminger. *Screenplay:* Siegfried Bernfeld, Arthur Berger. *Based on a true story.* *Photography:* Hans Theyer. *Sets:* Peter Herz. *Editor:* Paul Falkenberg. *Music:* Walter Landauer, Frank Fox. *Production:* Allianz Film GmbH Vienna, E.M.L.K. Wiessman Tonfilm. *Release:* Sud-Film A.G., December 21, 1931. 76 mins. *Players:* Hansi Niese (*The Mother*), Attila Hörbiger (*Franz*), Betty Bird (*Anni Huber*), Hugo Thimig (*Chief of Police*), Ferdinand Maierhofer (*Herr Huber*), Maria Waldner (*Frau Huber*), Hans Olden (*Dr. Steinlechner*), Adrienne Gessner (*Rosa*), Franz Engel, Georg Denes, Karl Goetz.

Story

Vienna, ten years after the war. A man returns from Russia to find his mother dead. A woman believes him to be her own son and takes him into her home. In order to give the man a future, she breaks the law, fortunately without serious consequences. However, there is no longer any doubt. The man is not her son, but their friendship continues.

Preminger: See page 40.

UNDER YOUR SPELL. 1936. *Director:* Otto Preminger. *Screenplay:* Frances Hyland, Saul Elkins. *Based on stories by:* Bernice Mason, Sy Bartlett. *Photography:* Sidney Wagner. *Editor:* Fred Allen. *Music and Lyrics:* Arthur Schwartz, Howard Dietz. *Musical Director:* Arthur Lange. *Associate Producer:* John Stone. *Release:* 20th. Century-Fox, April 11, 1936. 65 mins. *Players:* Lawrence Tibbett (*Anthony Allen*), Gregory Ratoff (*Petroff*), Wendy Barrie (*Cynthia Drexel*), Arthur Treacher (*Botts*), Gregory Gaye (*Count Paul of Rienne*), Berton Churchill (*The Judge*), Jed Prouty (*Mr. Twerp*), Charles Richman (*Uncle Bob*), Claudia Coleman (*Mrs. Twerp*).

Story

A concert singer retires to a ranch in order to get away from the impossible life imposed on him by his publicity agent. However, his newly-found peace is upset by the arrival of a spoiled young lady, whom he eventually ends up marrying.

Preminger: See page 43.

DANGER LOVE AT WORK. 1937. *Director:* Otto Preminger. *Screenplay:* James Edward Grant, Ben

Markson. *Based on a story by :* James Edward Grant. *Photography :* Virgil Miller. *Art Director :* Duncan Cramer. *Editor :* Jack Murray. *Music :* David Buttolph, *with Lyrics by :* Mack Gordon, Harry Revel. *Associate Producer :* Harold Wilson. *Release :* 20th. Century-Fox, September 30, 1937. 81 mins. *Players :* Ann Sothern (*Toni Pemberton*), Jack Haley (*Henry Mac Morrow*), Edward Everett Horton (*Howard Rogers*), Mary Boland (*Alice Pemberton*), Bennie Bartlett (*Pemberton Jr.*), Walter Catlett (*Uncle Alan*), John Carradine (*Herbert Pemberton*), Etienne Girardot (*Albert Pemberton*), Maurice Cass (*Uncle Goliath*), Alan Dinehart (*Allan Duncan*), E. E. Clive (*Wilbur*), Margaret McWade (*Aunt Patty*), Margaret Seddon (*Aunt Pitty*), Elisha Cook Jr. (*Druggist*), Hilda Vaughn (*The Pemberton's maid*), Charles Coleman (*Henry's servant*), George Chandler (*Attendant*), Spencer Charters (*Hick*), Hal K. Dawson (*Chauffeur*), Stanley Fields (*Thug*), Paul Hurst (*Policeman*), Claude Allister (*Salesman*), Jonathan Hale (*Parsons*), Charles Lane (*Gilroy*), Paul Stanton (*Hilton*).

Story

All the members of the Pemberton family are slightly crazy, with the exception of the daughter who is relatively normal. This daughter assists a young lawyer in obtaining the signatures of her parents for the sale of a piece of land, and she falls in love with the young man.

Preminger: See page 46.

MARGIN FOR ERROR. 1943. *Director :* Otto Preminger. *Screenplay :* Lillie Hayward. *Based on a play by :* Claire Boothe Luce. *Photography :* Edward Cronjager. *Art Directors :* Richard Day, Lewis Creber. *Set Directors :* Thomas Little, Al Orenbach. *Editor :* Louis Loeffler. *Musical Director :* Emil Newman. *Wardrobe Designer :* Earl Luick. *Producer :* Ralph Dietrich. *Release :* 20th Century-Fox, January 8, 1943. 74 mins. *Players :* Joan Bennett (*Sophie Baumer*), Milton Berle (*Moe Finkelstein*), Otto Preminger (*Karl Baumer*), Carl Esmond (*Baron Max von Alvenstor*), Howard Freeman (*Otto Hurst*), Poldy Dur (*Frieda*), Clyde Fillmore (*Dr. Jennings*), Joe Kirk (*Salomon*), Hans von Twardowski (*Fritz*), Ted North, Elmer Jack Semple, J. Norton Dunn (*The Saboteurs*), Hans Schumm (*Kurt Moeller*), Ed McNamara (*Captain Mulrooney*), Selmer Jackson (*Coroner*), Ferike Boros.

Story

A *Jewish detective is given responsibility for the protection of the German consul in an American city. The consul is a man who has been tyrannising both his wife as well as the staff of the consulate. While one of Hitler's speeches is coming over the*

Frank Latimore with Jeanne Crain, and Eugene Pallette at right, in IN THE MEANTIME DARLING

radio, the consul is found murdered. Finally, it is discovered that he was accidentally killed while attempting to murder his wife's lover.

Preminger: See pages 51, 53.

IN THE MEANTIME DARLING.

1944. *Director:* Otto Preminger. *Screenplay:* Arthur Kober, Michael Uris. *Photography:* Joe MacDonald. *Art Directors:* James Basevi, John Ewing. *Set Directors:* Thomas Little, Fred J. Rode. *Special Visual Effects:* Fred Sersen. *Editor:* Louis R. Loeffler. *Music:* David Buttolph. *Musical Director:* Emil Newman. *Wardrobe Designer:* Bonnie Cashin. *Choreography:* Geneva Sawyer. *Producer:* Otto Preminger. *Release:* 20th. Century-Fox, September 22, 1944. 72 mins. *Players:* Jeanne Crain (*Maggie Preston*), Frank Latimore (*Lt. Daniel Ferguson*), Mary Nash (*Mrs. Preston*), Eugene Pallette (*H. B. Preston*), Stanley Prager (*Lt. Philip "Red" Pianatowski*), Gale Robbins (*Shirley Pianatowski*), Jane Randolph (*Jerry Armstrong*), Doris Merrick (*Mrs. MacAndrews*), Cara Williams (*Mrs. Sayre*), Anne Corcoran (*Mrs. Bennett*), Reed Hadley (*Major Phillips*), Heather Angel (*Mrs. Nelson*), Bonnie Bannon (*Mrs. Farnum*), William Colby (*Lt. Farnum*), Cliff Clark (*Col. Corkery*), Elisabeth Risdon (*Mrs. Corkery*), Marjorie Masson (*Mrs. Cook*), Lee Bennett, Roger Clark, Lee March, Ruth Clifford, Frank Wilcox, Glenn Langan, Clarence Muse, Blake Edwards, Mary McCarty, Olin Howlin, Evelyn Mulhall, Geraldine Wall, Don Hayden, Lilian Bronson, Eddie Acuff, Merrill Rodin, Janet Burston, Paul Harvey, Milton Kibbee, Marvin Davis, Charles Hayes, Frank McLure, B. S. Pully.

Story

In order to be near her husband, who is in an army training camp, a young woman moves into lodgings occupied by wives of soldiers. She begins to realise how little she and her husband know of each other. Having quarrelled bitterly, they come to a reconciliation while the husband is on leave.

Preminger: See pages 53, 70.

LAURA. 1944. *Director :* Otto Preminger. *Screenplay :* Jay Dratler, Samuel Hoffenstein, Betty Reinhardt. *Based on a novel by :* Vera Casparay. *Photography :* Joseph La Shelle. *Art Directors :* Lyle R. Wheeler, Leland Fuller. *Set Directors :* Thomas Little, Paul S. Fox. *Special Visual Effects :* Fred Sersen. *Editor :* Louis R. Loeffler. *Music :* David Raksin. *Musical Director :* Emil Newman. *Wardrobe Designer :* Bonnie Cashin. *Producer :* Otto Preminger. *Release :* 20th. Century-Fox, October 17, 1944. 88 mins. *Players :* Gene Tierney (*Laura Hunt*), Dana Andrews (*Mark McPherson*), Clifton Webb (*Waldo Lydecker*), Vincent Price (*Shelby Carpenter*), Judith Anderson (*Anne Treadwell*), Dorothy Adams (*Bessie Clary*), James Flavin (*McAvity*), Clyde Fillmore (*Bullitt*), Ralph Dunn (*Fred Callahan*), Grant Mitchell (*Corey*), Kathleen Howard (*Louise*), Lee Tung Foo, Cy Kendall, Harold Schlickenmayer, Harry Strang, Lane Chandler.

Story

A body, with the face destroyed by a shot-gun blast, is found outside the flat of Laura Hunt, and the police assume that it is hers. Mark McPherson, a detective, visits Waldo Lydecker, a critic, who was a friend of Laura's.

Waldo is unhelpful but remarks that he is the only person that understood Laura. Mark next visits Anne Treadwell, Laura's wealthy aunt. She tells him that she has been having an affair with Shelby Carpenter, even though he is engaged to be married to Laura. Mark returns to Waldo who tells him that Laura had gone to her country home to decide whether to marry Shelby or not. He also learns that Waldo and Laura have been close friends for a long time and that Waldo had used his power as a critic to ridicule other men whom she found attractive. Laura met Shelby and became engaged to him though Waldo proved to her that he was having an affair with Diane Redfern, a model. Mark goes to Laura's flat and while he is there Laura walks

Dana Andrews in LAURA

81

in. She tells him that she has spent the weekend in the country and when she finds a dress belonging to Diane Redfern it becomes apparent that she is the disfigured victim. Leaving strict orders that she must contact no-one, Mark departs. Laura telephones Shelby but Mark, who has had her telephone tapped, follows him to Laura's flat where he forces the truth from him.

While Laura was away, Shelby had met Diane Redfern at the flat. They had been disturbed by a ring at the door and Diane had gone to answer while Shelby had hidden in the bedroom. He had heard a shot, seen the body and then fled.

Waldo enters and faints at the sight of Laura. Mark then arrests Laura and takes her to the police station. However, he assures her that he believes her to be innocent and then takes her home. He drives to Waldo's house and, finding him out, goes back to Laura's flat and confronts him there. Waldo becomes jealous of Mark and, after an argument, leaves. Mark finds the shot-gun in a grandfather clock and then explains to Laura that Waldo hid it there after the murder. Waldo had become very jealous of her affair with Shelby and had meant to kill her, not Diane. Mark leaves Laura alone and Waldo returns. He is just about to shoot her when Mark bursts in and shoots him dead with his revolver.

Preminger: See pages 55, 61.

ROYAL SCANDAL (British title: **CZARINA**). 1945. *Director:* Otto Preminger. *Screenplay:* Edwin Justus Mayer. *Adapted by:* Bruno Frank *from the play* "Czarina" *by:* Lajos Biro, Melchior Lengyel. *Photography:* Arthur Miller. *Art Directors:* Lyle R. Wheeler, Mark Lee Kirk. *Set Directors:* Thomas Little, Paul Fox. *Special Visual Effects:* Fred Sersen. *Editor:* Dorothy Spencer. *Music:* Alfred Newman *with orchestration by:* Edward Powell. *Wardrobe Designer:* René Hubert. *Producer:* Ernst Lubitsch. *Release:* 20th. Century-Fox, March 26, 1945. 94 mins. *Players:* Tallulah Bankhead (*Catherine II*), Charles Coburn (*Chancellor Nicolai Ilyitch*), Anne Baxter (*Countess Anna Jaschikoff*), William Eythe (*Lt. Alexis Chernoff*), Vincent Price (*Marquis de Fleury*), Sig Ruman (*General Ronsky*), Mischa Auer (*Captain Sukov*), Vladimir Sokoloff (*Malakoff*), Mikhail Rasumny (*Drunken General*), Grady Sutton (*Boris*), Don Douglas (*Variatinsky*), Egon Brecher (*Wassilikov*), Eva Gabor (*Countess Demidow*).

Story

Based on a very old stage play, The Czarina, *which had variously inspired a couple of previous pictures, including* Elisabeth Bergner's Catherine the Great, *this contemplation of the lady tells of one of her amorous adventures with a handsome young Guards cap-*

A ROYAL SCANDAL: Charles Coburn, William Eythe, and Tallulah Bankhead

tain. Intertwined with a modest boudoir story, in which the gentleman is bashful and pursued, is a plot about a palace revolution.

Preminger: See page 70.

FALLEN ANGEL. 1945. *Director:* Otto Preminger. *Screenplay:* Harry Kleiner. *Based on a novel by:* Marty Holland. *Photography:* Joseph La Shelle. *Art Directors:* Lyle R. Wheeler, Leland Fuller. *Set Directors:* Thomas Little, Helen Mansard. *Special Visual Effects:* Fred Sersen. *Editor:* Harry Reynolds. *Music:* David Raksin. *Musical Director:* Emil Newman. *The Song* "Slowly" *by:* David Raksin *with lyrics by:* Kermit Goell. *Wardrobe Designer:* Bonnie Cashin. *Producer:* Otto Preminger. *Release:* 20th. Century-Fox, November 7, 1945. 97 mins. *Players:* Dana Andrews (*Eric Stanton*), Alice Faye (*June Mills*), Linda Darnell (*Stella*), Charles Bickford (*Mark Judd*), Anne Revere (*Clara Mills*), Bruce Cabot (*Dave Atkins*), John Carradine (*Professor Madley*), Percy Kilbride (*Pop*), Olin Howlin (*Joe Ellis*), Jimmy Conlin (*Receptionist*), Hal Taliaferro, Mira McKinney, Guss Glassmire, Leila McIntyre, Garry Owen, Horace Murphy, Martha Wentworth, Paul Palmer, Paul Burns, Herb Ashley, Stymie Beard, William Hade, Chick Collins, Dorothy Adams, Harry Strang, Max Wagner, Broderick O'Farrell.

Story

Eric Stanton arrives at the small town of Walton with only one dollar. Taking advantage of a spiritualist who is in town, he begs a bed for the night and also meets and charms June Mills, a rich young lady who is the daughter of the late Mayor. He goes to a café to eat and falls in love with Stella the waitress. She is very bored with her way of life and agrees to marry Eric if he will provide her with money and a good home. Eric decides that he will marry June, get her money and then divorce her. He begins to court June who has led a sheltered life and is completely taken in by his charm. She falls in love with him

*Alice Faye and Dana Andrews in
FALLEN ANGEL*

and a secret marriage takes place.

On his wedding night Eric goes to
Stella to tell her of his success but she
will have nothing to do with him and
goes off to meet another man. During
the night Stella is murdered and Eric
sees himself as the obvious suspect. He
decides to try to evade the police and
June insists on coming with him, despite
the fact that her sister Clara has told
her of Eric's relationship with Stella.
They go to San Francisco where June
is arrested and questioned by Mark
Judd, a police inspector. However, she
will not tell him where Eric is.

Eric returns to the café in Walton
and finds Judd sitting there. Judd
arrests Eric but, while he is driving him
to the police station, Eric tells him that
he has discovered that he too was
Stella's lover. Judd admits that he
killed her by accident after a quarrel,
but as Eric can now prove him the
murderer, he decides to shoot him and
say that he was trying to escape. A
struggle takes place and Eric knocks
Judd unconscious, takes him to the
police station and returns to June,
whom he now loves deeply.

Preminger: See pages 74–75.

CENTENNIAL SUMMER. 1946.
Director: Otto Preminger. *Screen-
play:* Michael Kanin. *Based on the
novel by:* Albert E. Idell. *Photo-
graphy:* Ernest Palmer. *Art Direc-
tors:* Lyle R. Wheeler, Leland Fuller.
Editor: Harry Reynolds. *Music:*
Jerome Kern. *Musical Director:* Al-
fred Newman. *Songs and music by:*
Jerome Kern. *Lyrics by:* Oscar Ham-
merstein II "All through the Day";
Leo Robin "In Love in Vain," "Up
with the Lark," "Railroad Song,"
"Centennial Reprise," "The Light
Romance," "Concerto Piece," Happy
Anniversary," "Free America"; E. Y.
Harburg "Cinderella Sue." *Tech-
nicolor Advisors:* Natalie Kalmus,
Richard Mueller. *Wardrobe Designer:*
René Hubert. *Producer:* Otto Pre-
minger. *Release:* 20th Century-Fox,
May 29, 1946. 103 mins. *Players:*
Linda Darnell (*Edith Rogers*), Jeanne
Crain (*Julia Rogers*), Cornel Wilde
(*Philippe Lascalles*), William Eythe

(*Benjamin Franklin Phelps*), Walter Brennan (*Jesse Rogers*), Constance Bennett (*Zenia Lascalles*), Dorothy Gish (*Harriet Rogers*), Barbara Whiting (*Susanna Rogers*), Larry Stevens (*Richard Lewis*), Kathleen Howard (*Deborah*), Buddy Swan (*Dudley Rogers*), Charles Dingle (*Snodgrass*), Gavin Gordon (*Trowbridge*), Avon Long, Eddie Dunn, Lois Austin, Harry Strang, France Morris, Reginald Sheffield, William Frambes, Paul Everton, James Metcalfe, John Farrell, Robert Malcom, Billy Wayne, Edna Holland, Ferris Taylor, Winifred Harris, Rodney Bell, Clancy Cooper.

Story

In the summer of 1876, the centenary of the Declaration of Independence, the Rogers family are visited by their gay Aunt Zenia from Paris. She brings with her Philippe, a young Frenchman who is to organise the French contribution to the centenary exhibition being held in Philadelphia. Both the elder girls, Edith and Julia, are very impressed with him, despite the fact that Edith is engaged to Ben, a young doctor. The family go to the exhibition where they find Philippe in a very confused state. Julia helps him with his problems, acting as his interpreter, and romance begins to blossom, much to the annoyance of the scheming Edith.

Aunt Zenia, meanwhile, has set her cap at Jesse Rogers, the father of the family. She is determined that he will kiss at least one other woman other than his wife in the course of his life, but Harriet struggles valiantly to keep her husband faithful. Edith, in an attempt to win Philippe's affections, tells him that Julia is engaged to Ben. Philippe is distressed to hear this but decides to take on Edith as a consolation. Julia is confused by Philippe's actions but, seeing that the French pavilion will not do very well, she devises and organises a masked ball which is greatly successful. During the course of the ball the various members of the family become reconciled and are re-united with their proper partners.

Preminger: See pages 75–76.

Cornel Wilde with Walter Brennan (seated) in CENTENNIAL SUMMER

85

FOREVER AMBER. 1947. *Director:* Otto Preminger. *Screenplay:* Philip Dunne, Ring Lardner Jr. *Adapted by:* Jerome Cady *from the novel by:* Kathleen Windsor. *Photography:* Leon Shamroy. *Art Director:* Lyle R. Wheeler. *Set Directors:* Thomas Little, Walter M. Scott. *Special Visual Effects:* Fred Sersen. *Editor:* Louis R. Loeffler. *Music:* David Raksin. *Musical Director:* Alfred Newman *with orchestration by:* Maurice De Packh, Herbert Spencer. *Technicolor Advisors:* Natalie Kalmus, Richard Mueller. *Wardrobe Designers:* Charles Le Maire, René Hubert. *Fencing Master:* Fred Cavens. *Historical Consultant:* Dr. Godfrey Davies. *Producer:* William Perlberg. *Release:* 20th. Century-Fox, October 10, 1947. 140 mins. *Players:* Linda Darnell (*Amber St. Clair*), Cornel Wilde (*Bruce Carlton*), Richard Greene (*Lord Almsbury*), George Sanders (*Charles II*), Glenn Langan (*Captain Rex Morgan*), Richard Haydn (*Lord Radcliffe*), John Russell (*Black Jack Mallard*), Jane Ball (*Corinne Carlton*), Leo G. Carroll (*Matt Goodgroome*), Jessica Tandy (*Nan Britton*), Anne Revere (*Mother Red Cap*), Robert Coote (*Sir Thomas Dudley*), Natalie Draper (*Countess of Castlemaine*), Margaret Wycherley (*Mrs. Spong*), Alma Kruger (*Lady Redmond*), Edmond Breon (*Lord Redmond*), Alan Napier (*Landale*).

Story

At the time of the Stuart Restoration, Amber St. Clair, a beautiful peasant girl, falls in love with Lord Carlton and follows him to London where she becomes his mistress. Carlton, however, angers the King by being a little too attentive to Lady Castlemaine, the royal favourite, and is ordered to leave the country.

Deprived of the protection of her lover, Amber is soon behind the bars of the debtor's prison. She quickly escapes with the assistance of her new lover, a highwayman called Black Jack Mallard, and it is at his hideout that she gives birth to Lord Carlton's son. She then embarks upon a life of crime, luring men into alleys so that Black Jack and her confederates may rob them. Black Jack is eventually killed by the law and Amber takes refuge in the arms of Captain Rex Morgan who finds her a job at the Drury Lane Theatre.

Lord Carlton returns and visits her, but Morgan challenges him to a duel and, although the former is the victor, he is forced to flee abroad. Amber marries the elderly Lord Radcliffe, who takes her to the court of King Charles. The King is intrigued by Amber, but, not wishing to be cuckolded, Radcliffe takes her away and instals her in his London house. Carlton returns again to London and catches the Plague. Amber nurses him back to health, but when he learns of her marriage, he sails off to

America. Lord Radcliffe perishes in the great fire of London and Amber becomes the mistress of the King. When Carlton, now married, returns again and ignores her, Amber tries to trick the King into compromising his wife so that he will return to her. This fails and the King banishes Amber from the court. The final blow is struck when Carlton takes his son away from Amber leaving her completely alone.

Preminger: See pages 63, 73.

DAISY KENYON. 1947. *Director:* Otto Preminger. *Screenplay:* David Hertz. *Based on the novel by:* Elizabeth Janeway. *Photography:* Leon Shamroy. *Art Directors:* Lyle R. Wheeler, George Davis. *Set Directors:* Thomas Little, Walter M. Scott. *Special Visual Effects:* Fred Sersen. *Editor:* Louis Loeffler. *Music:* David Raksin. *Musical Director:* Alfred Newman *with orchestration by:* Herbert Spencer. *Wardrobe Designer:* Charles Le Maire. *Producer:* Otto Preminger. *Release:* 20th. Century-Fox, November 27, 1947. 99 mins. *Players:* Joan Crawford (*Daisy Kenyon*), Dana Andrews (*Dan O'Mara*), Henry Fonda (*Peter Lapham*), Ruth Warrick (*Lucille O'Mara*), Peggy Ann Garner (*Rosamund O'Mara*), Connie Marshall (*Mariette O'Mara*), Martha Stewart (*Mary Angelus*), Nicholas Joy (*Coverly*), Art Baker (*Lucille's lawyer*), Robert Karnes (*Lawyer*),

DAISY KENYON: above, Joan Crawford with Henry Fonda; below, with Dana Andrews

John Davidson (*Mervyn*), Charles Meredith (*Judge*), Roy Roberts (*Dan's lawyer*), Griff Barnett (*Thompson*), Tito Vuolo (*Dino*), Victoria Horne (*Marsha*), George E. Stone (*Waiter*), Walter Winchell, Leonard Lyons, John Garfield, Fernando Lamas (*Stork Club Patrons*).

Story

A Triangle Drama . . . Daisy Kenyon, a fashion designer, decides that her affair with Dan O'Mara, a lawyer and a married man with two daughters, must come to an end. She meets and subsequently marries Peter Lapham, a U.S. Army Sergeant, but a yacht designer in civil life. They leave New York for a small seaside village and are ideally happy.

Back in New York to finish a magazine assignment, Daisy is visited by Dan, who is still in love with her. His wife listens in to a telephone conversation which follows between them and starts divorce proceedings, naming Daisy as co-respondent.

When the case is called off and Dan has thought of another way to get Daisy to return to him, she makes her final decision, and Peter reminds Dan that after all he is her husband.

Preminger: I don't remember the film at all.

THAT LADY IN ERMINE. 1948. *Director:* Otto Preminger. *Screenplay:* Samson Raphaelson. *Based on an operetta by:* Rudolph Schanzer and E. Welisch. *Photography:* Leon Shamroy. *Art Directors:* Lyle R. Wheeler, J. Russell Spencer. *Set Directors:* Thomas Little, Walter M. Scott. *Special Visual Effects:* Fred Sersen. *Editor:* Dorothy Spencer. *Music and Lyrics:* Leo Robin and Frederick Hollander, "This Is the Moment," "There's Something about the Midnight," "Oooh! What I'll do." *Musical Director:* Alfred Newman *with orchestration by:* Edward Powell, Herbert Spencer, Maurice De Packh. *Choreography:* Hermes Pan. *Wardrobe Designer:* René

Betty Grable with Cesar Romero in
THE LADY IN ERMINE

Hubert. *Producer:* Ernst Lubitsch. *Release:* 20th. Century-Fox, July 15, 1948. 89 mins. *Players:* Betty Grable (*Angelina and Francesca*), Douglas Fairbanks Jr. (*Col. Ladislas Karolyi Teglash and the Duke*), Virginia Campbell (*Theresa*), Cesar Romero (*Mario*), Walter Abel (*Major Horvath and Benvenuto*), Reginald Gardiner (*Alberto*), Harry Davenport (*Luigi*), Whit Bissell (*Guilio*), Edmund MacDonald (*Captain Novak*), David Bond (*Gabor*), Harry Cording, Belle Mitchell, Mary Bear, Jack George, John Parrish, Mayo Newhall (*Ancestors*), Lester Allen (*Jester*).

Story

Countess Angelina, the ruler of a small European country, is about to be married to Mario, her love, when the country is invaded by Colonel Ladislas Teglash. The Colonel takes over the country and instals himself in Countess Angelina's castle. Mario, meanwhile, rather than stay and defend his betrothed, has fled disguised as a gypsy. One night, Angelina's ancestors step down from their pictures and tell her about one of her predecessors who, in a similar predicament, married the invader in exchange for the freedom of her country and then stabbed him to death in his sleep. The beautiful Angelina marries Colonel Ladislas and her subjects are liberated. Instead of murdering him, however, she falls in love with him and promises him to be a true wife.

Preminger: See page 72.

THE FAN (British title: **LADY WINDERMERE'S FAN**). 1949. *Director:* Otto Preminger. *Screenplay:* Walter Reisch, Dorothy Parker, Ross Evans. *Based on the play* "Lady Windermere's Fan" *by:* Oscar Wilde (previously adapted for the cinema by Ernst Lubitsch in 1925). *Photography:* Joseph La Shelle. *Art Directors:* Lyle R. Wheeler, Leland Fuller. *Set Directors:* Thomas Little, Paul S. Fox. *Special Visual Effects:* Fred

George Sanders (left) in THE FAN

Sersen. *Editor:* Louis R. Loeffler. *Music:* Daniele Amfitheatrof. *Music Director:* Alfred Newman *with orchestration by:* Edward Powell, Maurice de Packh. *Wardrobe Designers:* Charles Le Maire, René Hubert. *Producer:* Otto Preminger. *Release:* 20th Century-Fox, April 7, 1949. 79 mins. *Players:* Jeanne Crain (*Lady Windermere*), Madeleine Carroll (*Mrs. Erlynne*), George Sanders (*Lord Darlington*), Richard Greene (*Lord Windermere*), Martita Hunt (*Duchess of Berwick*), John Sutton (*Cecil Graham*), Hugh Dempster (*Lord Augustus Lorton*), Richard Ney (*Mr. Hopper*), Virginia McDowall (*Lady Agatha*), Hugh Murray (*Dawson*), Frank Elliott (*The Jeweller*), John Burton (*Hoskins*), Trevor Ward (*The Auctioneer*), Patricia Walker (*An American*), Eric Noonan (*Underwood*), Winifred Harris (*The Maid*), Alphonse Martell (*Philippe*), Felippa Rock (*Rosalie*), Colin Campbell (*The Tailor*), Terry Kilburn (*A Messenger*), Tempe Pigott (*Mrs. Rudge*).

Story

Mrs. Erlynne, an attractive social climber, comes to London and forces her attentions upon Lord Windermere. Taking advantage of the fact that Lord Lorton is in love with her, she uses him to get to Lord Windermere. Having cornered Lord Windermere, she brazenly insists that he should let her live in one of his Mayfair properties and that he should pay all her bills.

The Windermeres give a ball and it is there that Lady Windermere confides her suspicions and distress to Lord Darlington, who secretly loves her. He, seeing a fine opportunity to win her for himself, begs her to run away with him. Lady Windermere considers Lord Darlington's proposition and then leaves the ball and goes to his house. Worried at what is going on, Mrs. Erlynne follows her there and a confrontation takes place. It comes to light that Mrs. Erlynne is really Lady Windermere's long lost mother and that her behaviour with Lord Windermere was just a way of getting close to her daughter. At this point they hear Lords Windermere, Darlington and Lorton entering the house and run to hide. Lord Windermere discovers his wife's fan, which she dropped in her hurry to conceal herself, and angrily demands to search the house. Lord Darlington refuses and the two men fight; meanwhile the two women slip quietly away. Mrs. Erlynne returns to the house with the aim of restoring peace and claims Lady Windermere's fan, explaining that she took it by mistake and that it was she who left it at Lord Darlington's house. Mrs. Erlynne then leaves for Paris, taking with her the fan as a token of gratitude from her daughter. Lord and Lady Windermere continue to live in marital bliss until they finally *die together when a bomb falls on their house during the* Blitz.

Preminger: Lubitsch had made *The Fan* in 1925, and I admit it was a mistake on my part to have re-made this play. Whatever I did to the film was wrong. It is one of the few pictures I disliked while I was working on it. More than this I don't remember.

WHIRLPOOL. 1949. *Director :* Otto Preminger. *Screenplay :* Ben Hecht (under the pseudonym Lester Bartow), Andrew Solt. *Based on a novel by :* Guy Endore. *Photography :* Arthur Miller. *Art Directors :* Lyle R. Wheeler, Leland Fuller. *Set Directors :* Thomas Little, Walter M. Scott. *Special Effects :* Fred Sersen. *Editor :* Louis R. Loeffler. *Music :* David Raksin. *Musical Director :* Alfred Newman *with orchestration by :* Edward Powell. *Technical Advisors for Hypnotism Scenes :* Dr. H. A. Conway, Cora Presser. *Wardrobe Designers :* Charles Le Maire, Oleg Cassini (for Gene Tierney). *Producer :* Otto Preminger. *Release :* 20th Century-Fox, November 28, 1949. 97 mins. *Players :* Gene Tierney (*Ann Sutton*), Richard Conte (*Dr. William Sutton*), José Ferrer (*David Korvo*), Charles Bickford (*Lt. Colton*), Barbara O'Neil (*Theresa Randolph*), Eduard Franz (*Martin Avery*), Constance Collier (*Tina Cosgrove*), Fortunio Bonanova (*Feruccio di Ravallo*),

Ruth Lee (*Miss Hall*), Ian MacDonald (*Detective Hogan*), Bruce Hamilton (*Lt. Jeffreys*), Alex Gerry (*Dr. Peter Duval*), Larry Keating (*Mr. Simms*), Mauritz Hugo (*Hotel Employee*), John Trebach (*Freddie*), Myrtle Anderson (*Agnes*), Larry Dobkin (*Surgeon Wayne*), Jane Van Duser (*Miss Andrews*), Nancy Valentine (*Taffy Lou*), Clancy Cooper, Eddie Dunn (*Two Policemen in the final scene*), Randy Stuart (*Miss Landau*), Helen Westcott (*The Secretary*), Mack Williams (*Whorton*), Howard Negley (*Gordon*), Robert Foulk (*Andy*), Charles J. Flynn (*A Policeman*), Phyllis Hill (*Cocktail Party Guest*).

Jose Ferrer with Gene Tierney in WHIRLPOOL

Story

   Ann Sutton, a wealthy psychiatrist's wife, suffers from insomnia and kleptomania. Korvo, who practices astrology and hypnotism, rescues her from the consequences of stealing a brooch from a shop and persuades her to be treated by him.

   Korvo is being threatened by an ex-mistress whom he has tricked out of a large sum of money. He hypnotises Ann and sends her to the woman's house (having first arranged incriminating evidence) so that she is caught beside the dead body and arrested.

   Korvo himself, recovering in hospital from an operation, has an apparently unshakable alibi. The psychiatrist believes that Korvo has hypnotised himself, so gaining strength to leave the hospital and commit the murder. The detective takes his prisoner to the scene of the crime for the psychiatrist to attempt a reconstruction. Korvo, again under hypnosis, has gone there to try to recover evidence against himself, is caught, and dies from loss of blood.

Preminger: I cannot remember anything about this film.

WHERE THE SIDEWALK ENDS. 1950. *Director:* Otto Preminger. *Screenplay:* Rex Conner. *Based on an adaptation by:* Victor Trivas, Frank P. Rosenberg, Robert E. Kent *of a novel by:* William L. Stuart. *Photography:* Joseph La Shelle. *Art Directors:* Lyle R. Wheeler, J. Russell Spencer. *Set Directors:* Thomas Little, Walter M. Scott. *Special Effects:* Fred Sersen. *Editor:* Louis Loeffler. *Music:* Cyril Mockridge. *Musical Director:* Lionel Newman *with orchestration by:* Edward Powell. *Wardrobe Designers:* Charles Le Maire, Oleg Cassini (for Gene Tierney). *Producer:* Otto Preminger. *Release:* 20th. Century-Fox, June 26, 1950. 95 mins. *Players:* Dana Andrews (*Mark Dixon*), Gene Tierney (*Morgan Taylor*), Gary Merrill (*Scalise*), Bert Freed (*Paul Klein*), Tom Tully (*Jiggs Taylor*), Karl Malden (*Lt. Bill Thomas*), Ruth Donnelly (*Martha*), Craig Stevens (*Ken Payne*), Robert F. Simon (*Inspector Nicholas Foley*), Harry Von Zell (*Ted Morrison*), Don Appell (*Willie*), Neville Brand (*Steve*), Grace Mills (*Mrs. Tribaum*), Lou Krugman (*Mike Williams*), David McMahon (*Harrington*), David Wolfe (*Sid Kramer*), Steve Roberts (*Gilruth*), Phil Tully (*Tod Benson*), Ian MacDonald (*Casey*), John Close (*Hanson*), John McGuire (*Gertessen*), Lou Nova (*Ernie*), Ralph Peters (*Counterman*),

Gene Tierney and Dana Andrews in
WHERE THE SIDEWALK ENDS

Oleg Cassini (*Mayer*), Louise Lorimer (*Mrs. Jackson*), Lester Sharpe (*Friedman*), Chili Williams (*Teddy*), Robert Foulk (*Feeney*), Eda Reiss Merin (*Mrs. Klein*), Mack Williams (*Morris*), Duke Watson (*Taxi Driver*), Clancy Cooper (*Lt. Arnaldo*), Bob Evans (*Sweatshirt*), Joseph Granby (*Fat man*), Charles J. Flynn (*Schwartz*), Larry Thomson (*Riley*), Fred Graham (*Attendant*), Robert B. Williams (*A Policeman*).

Story

A tough policeman with a reputation for beating confessions out of criminals is sent to question a man suspected of murder, becomes involved in a fight, and accidentally kills him. He believes that a gang leader, Scalise, is responsible for the original crime, and that if he succeeds in concealing his own guilt he can secure Scalise's conviction for both murders.

Unfortunately he meets and falls in love with his victim's widow, only to find that her father is accused of his own crime. The policeman then decides to sacrifice himself by deliberately provoking the gang to kill him, leaving a letter for the police that will ensure their conviction for his own death.

Instead, he traps the gang singlehanded, and is congratulated by the police inspector ; but now, moved by love rather than the wish to conceal his crime, he confesses. He is sent up for trial, but we are left to assume that the ending will be a happy one.

Preminger: I remember nothing about it.

THE THIRTEENTH LETTER. 1950. *Director :* Otto Preminger. *Screenplay :* Howard Koch. *Based on a script by :* Louis Chavance for *Le Corbeau* (H. G. Clouzot, 1943). *Photography :* Joseph La Shelle. *Art Directors :* Lyle R. Wheeler, Maurice Ransford. *Set Directors :* Thomas Little, Walter M. Scott. *Special Effects :* Fred Sersen. *Editor :* Louis Loeffler. *Music :* Alex North. *Musical Director :* Lionel Newman *with orchestration by :* Maurice De Packh. *Wardrobe Designers :* Charles Le Maire, Edward Stevenson. *Producer :*

THE THIRTEENTH LETTER

Otto Preminger. *Release :* 20th Century-Fox, January 19, 1951. 85 mins. (Exteriors filmed in Quebec, Canada.) *Players :* Linda Darnell (*Denise Tourneur*), Charles Boyer (*Dr. Paul Laurent*), Michael Rennie (*Dr. Pearson*), Constance Smith (*Cora Laurent*), Françoise Rosay (*Mrs. Simms*), Judith Evelyn (*Sister Mary*), Guy Sorel (*Robert Helier*), June Hedin (*Rochelle*), Paul Guevremont (*Postman*), George Alexander (*Dr. Fletcher*), J. Leo Gagnon (*Dr. Helier*), Ovila Legare (*The Mayor*), Camille Ducharme (*Fredette*).

Story

A study of the effects of an outbreak of poison-pen letters in a small Canadian town. The first is about the relationship of a young doctor at the hospital with the senior doctor's wife. Others follow, until almost all the main figures in the town are involved in one way or another. Suspicion falls on a sister at the hospital, she is arrested, the letters stop, the town begins to recover, and then . . . a new flood starts.

A local boy in hospital gets a letter telling him he has cancer — he commits suicide. During the funeral, a letter drops out of the wreath. A handwriting test is carried out and a young hypochondriac who is in love with the doctor is suspected.

Eventually the mystery is traced to the senior doctor's wife who, under his influence, has been made to write the letters. Finally the suicide's mother visits the doctor and kills him; the wife is free at last, and the young doctor and the girl live happily.

Preminger: I liked the original film, I worked on the script of my version, I produced it, and if it is the same as the original I must have decided to do it this way. But I do not remember anything about the picture. You must remember that I detach myself completely from a film once it is finished. I will not live in the past. For me, it is over, I must go on to something new. Just the other day I looked at *In Harm's Way*. We made one small cut for television. It was like looking at someone else's picture.

ANGEL FACE. 1952. *Director*: Otto Preminger. *Screenplay*: Frank Nugent and Oscar Millard. *Based on a story by*: Chester Erskine. *Photography*: Harry Stradling. *Art Directors*: Albert S. D'Agostino, Carroll Clark. *Set Directors*: Darell Silvera, Jack Mills. *Editor*: Frederick Knudtson. *Music*: Dimitri Tiomkin. *Musical Director*: Constantin Bakaleinikoff. *Wardrobe Designer*: Michael Woulfe. *Producer*: Howard Hughes. *Release*: RKO, December 11, 1952. 90 mins. *Players*: Robert Mitchum (*Frank Jessup*), Jean Simmons (*Diane Tremayne*), Mona Freeman (*Mary Wilton*), Herbert Marshall (*Mr. Charles Tremayne*), Leon Ames (*Fred Barrett*), Barbara O'Neil (*Mrs. Catherine Tremayne*), Kenneth Tobey (*Bill Crompton*), Raymond Greenleaf (*Arthur Vance*), Griff Barnett (*The Judge*), Robert Gist (*Miller*), Jim Backus (*Judson*), Morgan Brown (*Harry the bartender*), Morgan Farley (*A Juror*), Herbert Lytton (*The Doctor*).

Story

Ambulance driver Frank Jessup is called out when the wealthy Mrs. Tremayne is found gassed. She recovers and claims that there was an attempt on her life. Frank becomes involved with the daughter, Diane. He throws over his fiancée and gets a job as the Tremaynes' chauffeur. Diane is devoted to her father and hates her step-mother, whom she accuses of trying to kill her. Frank becomes suspicious, but before he can get away, Diane murders Mrs. Tremayne by tampering with the car gears. The plan misfires, however, and her father also dies. Frank and Diane stand trial together for murder, but a smart lawyer insists that they marry before the trial, plays for sympathy and gets them off. When she finds that Frank means to have nothing more to do with her, Diane drives her own car backwards off the same cliff, killing both of them.

Preminger: See pages 41, 76.

Robert Mitchum and Jean Simmons in
ANGEL FACE

William Holden, Maggie McNamara and David Niven in THE MOON IS BLUE

PART TWO

OTTO PREMINGER—Independent Film-Maker
[In New York, 1956]

Being an independent producer indicates a change which I am convinced will go much further than it has so far, which developed during the last few years, the change from mass production by major studios to individual productions. Today, independent producers (like myself, Kazan, Wallis, Kramer) produce a picture like we produce plays on Broadway, which means selecting a subject, having a screenplay written, casting it, being autonomous; it is the individual's authority and his responsibility. He stands and falls with the success of this one picture. There is no supervision from any front office, there are no alibis that we used to have. If we had a bad cast, it was always Zanuck at 20th Century-Fox and Louis B. Mayer at M-G-M who were blamed. It was their fault, because naturally when running a big business, which a major studio company is, the head cannot worry about one individual picture. It was probably the right way to do mass production pictures, when people flocked into the theatre. People used to go to the movies. I don't think they go to the movies any more, not as indiscriminately as they used to. I think they go to see one particular movie, they select. Unless a picture has something special to offer the audience, to make people leave their homes, their televisions and go to the theatre, stand in line, buy their tickets, have all the inconveniences, park their cars, have bad weather, baby sitters, expenses, all these things, as opposed to the comfort of a living-room chair, or a television screen, and the possibility for one member of the family, usually it is the man, to read his newapaper, or not to watch, or to doze off, then they will not go out to the cinema. And in spite of the dreadful commercial interruptions, which provide breaks for refreshment and reading, television has all the shows, all the themes that the average picture used to have.

D

So what makes people decide to go and see a film? How will they know that this is a film for which they should go to all this trouble? *Look* magazine recently found out that less than ten per cent of people who go to the movies are influenced by what they read about a picture.

Well, people have instincts about what they want to see. This I experienced in my career as far back as 1935 when I landed here from Europe, when I did plays on Broadway, and early in the picture business—the public seems to have an instinct. This is best judged with Broadway plays. The usual Broadway play gets the same publicity, the same ads, two Sundays before opening. The box-office is opened for mail orders, and this is advertised. There is no big advertising campaign, because the money is not available as it is for movies. Now, with some openings on Broadway, and they do not necessarily have to be related to the star, the writer or the director, it is absolutely impossible, even if you know the people, to get tickets to the opening. They are gone before you know, and people are filling in mail orders, they want to see it. They know, they have an instinct for what they want to see. Other plays, which are equally advertised, I would say, can't get people even with free admission to come to the opening, even the opening already is half empty. Now there must be something. Is it word of mouth? The subject which comes through? The title? The chemistry of the whole? It is the same with movies. *From Here to Eternity* was based on a best seller, that is true, but it didn't have any unusual publicity, yet at eight o'clock that morning, when it opened here on Broadway, at the Capitol, I happened to walk by, and there was a line three blocks long to get into the theatre. The same company believed in another picture *The Long Gray Line*, and did tremendous advance publicity. The head of the company, Mr. Harry Cohn, told me "This is ten times better than *From Here to Eternity*," and he really believed in it. The publicity was backed by the conviction of everybody connected with this film that it was a great picture. So it was, but it didn't turn out too well. When they opened, the audiences didn't want to go.

There is something about a theme, it can't be described. There is magic about it, like there is magic about an audience. A thousand people go to see a play or a picture, and every individual might just be an average man, with no particular talent, brains, intelligence, taste. They can't even tell us what they like, what they want, and then they come together, they have one big brain, one big heart, one good taste, and they determine what is successful. That's why I believe in the public. I don't believe we can play down to the public.

The major studios still exist, and they still make a programme of twenty, or twenty-five or thirty pictures, but they really exist only by tricks, by the wide screen that they have brought in, and the by-products. They have found oil on their grounds, all of them have laboratories, distribution companies and films for television, so that by the end of the year, the whole operation seems successful when you look at the ledger. Actually if you compare in these very prosperous times the financial success of the movie "industry," as an "industry," with any other industry, you will find that it is very poor, that proportionally, they don't have anything; if supposedly there would be a financial and economic setback, I think the movies would go bankrupt right away, as an "industry." On the other hand, the individual successful movie (I don't even want to say the individual good movie, but the movie that people want to see) is *much* more successful, grosses much more money than ever before. In other words, in my opinion, television has done for pictures what the talking pictures did for the stage, made them special. You have to do it with more care, just like the stage . . . There used to be up to a hundred and fifty stage plays every season in New York, and naturally many of them were not so good; but they still ran before there were talking pictures. When the talking pictures came in, the standard of the plays went up. When we have a season of about ninety plays, about nine or ten are successful, and the other eighty are not living, but the popular plays are doing more business and have more audiences than ever before.

Television is not entirely to blame for the troubles of the studios, and those who say so are wrong. I think the decline has two starting points. One is television, but that alone would not have destroyed the power of the major studios. Their power was definitely at an end when the government won an anti-trust suit which divorced exhibition from production against the motion picture companies. In other words, until this suit, the major studios, or five of the major companies, as a matter of fact, controlled ninety per cent of all the theatres in the United States. Not only could a picture like *The Man with the Golden Arm* or my *The Moon Is Blue* (which did not get a production code Seal from the Motion Picture Producers' Association) not play in any of these theatres, because the theatres were also bound by that code, and by the Seal (so they could not block-book it), not only that, the influence of these major studios was so great that nobody would finance an independent producer, because it was very, very unlikely that he would get first-rate playing dates. All the good playing dates were given, and this is why the government felt that it was monopoly, to the films of the major studios, to major producers. Now, today this is different. The theatres are not owned by the studios. I have proven once, and am about to prove again, the Code Seal doesn't mean a thing, and you get bookings. As a matter of fact, I booked *The Man with the Golden Arm* in California in the former 20th Century-Fox chain, in Fox West Coast Theatres, which is one of the biggest theatre chains in the United States. I told the President, "I probably won't get the Seal." He said "I don't care, the Seal doesn't mean anything to me," and he booked the picture, because he liked it. Now this independence of exhibition made the independent producer possible, and this independence will go further.

Politically or strategically, the major picture producers make mistakes when they forbid a picture by withholding the Seal that eventually might play all these theatres, because then their lack of power becomes very evident. When I did *The Moon Is Blue*, a very good friend of mine, the head of a studio, called me into his office and said "Look, I will cut it for you. A few cuts and you will get the Seal." I said "I can't, I have made a public statement that I want to test my right as a citizen of the United States to show this picture to the

American public as I have done it." It is not on the pretence that this little comedy would suffer if I took out a few lines—that had nothing to do with it. I made it like this, and I want to show it like this. So he said "I guarantee you won't show it in more than five theatres, you will not get bookings." I said "We'll see." The picture played in something like eight or nine thousand theatres in the United States and grossed more than many pictures that this man produced in his major studio, with all the help of the big chains and everything, and he feels now, rather foolish. Mr. Geoffrey Shurlock (administrator of the Code) by the way, wanted to give the Seal to both pictures. He is a very liberal man, but he can't do it because he is an employee of the M.P.P.A. Now, the power is broken. People will tell you that *I Am a Camera* or *The Outlaw* couldn't be successful without the Seal. That is true, but they wouldn't have been successful with the Seal either. You see, this is the point. *I Am a Camera* would probably be an "art theatre" picture with or without the Seal. Some theatres use the lack of the Seal for publicity, as though the film were immoral. This is wrong. I think if the audience wants to see something, they find it, and if they don't want to see it, the Seal certainly doesn't matter, as the endless chain of unsuccessful major pictures produced in the last two years has proved.

Back in his screening room, 1970

Let me explain something to you about risks. I have been broke several times in my life, and very often it looked as though it was the end of my career. I have many flops and also many successes. I never think in these terms, and this is something I must explain about myself. I don't think about risks. Somehow, every day when we wake up, and get dressed, take a bath, go out, we take risks. On the other hand, the chances of survival are pretty good. I would say that risks are challenges, and I like to meet them, I don't worry about them. It is more interesting to me to make a film or to work on something which is a challenge, than to work at something which seems to be completely without risk, particularly in our business where usually the things which seem completely without risk turn out to be the great disappointments. The beautiful side to our profession is that everything is a "risk," because only the risks are worthwhile—try! Being aware, as I am at my age, that one's existence is to end sooner or later, worry about risks is futile. I like to live, I enjoy my life, I like particularly to live now as I have children, to help them to grow up, and be remembered. I love my wife; but I cannot get up every day and say: "My God, don't do this. If I make a wrong step something will happen." It's not my nature to worry. If it were my nature I would try to educate myself not to worry.

Look at the incidents in my career that made headlines. Today we wonder what the fuss was all about. Society changes. Our whole life was different. Today, on a radio programme, we say things we used not to say in mixed company. This also is only a form of life which changes, and by using the most outrageous language a few times, the most horrible words imaginable, the shock is over. What is shocking? Only the unusual, the unexpected. Once done, done twice, it's over. People who make so much fuss about nudity and sex shouldn't go to see it, if they don't like it. The shows would close. But people criticise, get on soap boxes and speak against it, and the public buy more tickets to see it. Why shouldn't they? If they want to see it, fine. As far as the Legion of Decency and *The Moon Is Blue* was concerned, my position was then, and is now, that I am not a Catholic. I think they have a right to tell their members what to see and what not to see, but not other people.

I made *Hurry Sundown* which was also condemned, like *The Moon Is Blue*. I have a friend, Father Lubbers, who is the head of the Art Department of the Catholic University of Omaha, Nebraska, the Creighton University. I met him by accident on Fifth Avenue. It is a very amusing story. I was walking to my office on Saturday, and this young, slim priest said: "You are Mr. Preminger, aren't you? Could you lend me sixty cents?" And I said: "Certainly, Father, what for?"

He replied: "I am sixty cents short of my bus fare to Omaha." He told me who he was, the head of the Art Department of this University, and I invited him to lunch. He did not accept one cent more than sixty cents. I said: "Have a couple of dollars and send it back to me." But he refused. Shortly after he came back, and invited me to lunch. By then I had finished *Hurry Sundown* and he said: "If we have a festival, will you show the film at the University." I said "I can't show the film because it's a Catholic University and it has been condemned by the Legion of Decency." He said: "We don't care what the Legion of Decency says." And he showed the film at the University, which has ninety-five per cent Catholic students, one hundred per cent Catholic faculty. He didn't care, he's this kind of a man. So this powerful group is not powerful. It is like other pressure groups, only as powerful as the power we give them. As far as production and administration was concerned, I did, as producer, try if possible to conform to their rules, but when they completely, arbitrarily, did not permit us to mention the problem of drugs I said, "this is ridiculous and old-fashioned."

Today, people everywhere ask me to lend them *The Man with the Golden Arm*, because they want to discuss drugs, they want to see it dramatised in public. That is the story of everything. If you don't challenge these rules, then the world doesn't move forward. That's why I admire some of the young people. Whether they are completely right in challenging the establishment today, and the world we have made for them, or whether they are wrong, or half right, or half wrong, they are mostly honest; they protest, they *mean* what they are doing, they want to be listened to. I think all these problems would be much easier, and there would be no so-called generation gaps, if all university presidents would act more wisely. My wife went to Smith, I think I told you. Her president sent a letter to the parents and *alumni* explaining how he handled a strike there. He acted with intelligence. The President of Berkeley did not. As a result the Governor of the State, Ronald Reagan, sent in the police, saying there must be law and order. The police in a free country, in a democracy, should

Frank Sinatra, John Conte, and Kim Novak in THE MAN WITH
THE GOLDEN ARM

arrest people and bring them before a court, not beat them up and
shoot them. It's wrong. These are the acts of totalitarian governments.

When I pass the Fox lot, today, I only think not to miss the red
light! That's all. I have no sentimental feeling. I had a good time,
partly, at Fox, but the past for me is past. I don't brood about it, I
don't think about it, or the mistakes that I made, or my achievements.
My joy is in living and living today, and particularly looking forward
to living tomorrow. The studios are falling apart. They are selling
their assets more and more, and eventually I think pictures will
probably have to be financed individually as plays are being financed,
and there will also be independent distribution. I don't know if I

would do it, if I want to bother. But, for instance, if I made a film and financed it independently, I wouldn't need all the machinery which now exists to distribute it. I could open it, let's say, in New York. If it's a flop, nothing helps. If it's a success, then very soon exhibitors all over the country will know this and come to me to buy it. The speed of communications today is so swift, people know everything that happens in their profession. Certainly in our profession everyone knows immediately when a film is a success. If a film opens in New York and you are in Toronto you know immediately about it, and you're not even interested, like an exhibitor, from the competitive business point of view. You are interested only because you write about films and you like them. But the theatre owners in Toronto would immediately start to bid for it. The system as it is today with all the bureaucracy and the thirty-six sales branches is not necessary.

It will all disappear soon, it is all old-fashioned. It started at a time when it took two or three hours to get a long-distance call from New York to Chicago, when there were no planes, no jets. How long is it to fly to Toronto today? Fifty minutes. How long did it take when the motion picture business started, fifty-five or sixty years ago? It took twenty-four hours. That's the difference which the business side of our profession hasn't caught up with. People who make clothes don't act like this. They invite buyers once or four times a year at different seasons, to New York or Chicago and show them their clothes and the buyers buy them, or won't buy them, and that's it. They don't have establishments everywhere, it would cost them money and it's not necessary. It will all change. It will be simplified, and besides this, it's not important.

What is important is to be able to make a film, to tell a story that is interesting, to have characters to identify with, to entertain people. When I say "entertain" I mean (I often say this) not only to make audiences laugh or cry, but to make them think. Stimulating people to deeper thought, to broaden their outlook on the world, is the greatest entertainment really. I think that *Hamlet* is much more entertaining than a comedy by Neil Simon; no matter how much we laugh at the comedy, there is something about Shakespeare that stays with us and the more often we see it the more it makes us think and feel. This is why Shakespeare is one of the greatest entertainers—whether it is film or drama. Shakespeare would have probably made films if there had been film at that time! This is only a question of the means being used, live actors or photographed actors. Entertainment is not just to say "ha, ha, ha." That in fact is probably the most passing entertainment—just to laugh. With a farce, no matter how much we laugh, we go home and it's gone. A very moving play—like *Hamlet* or *King Lear*—is unforgettable. I remember today most of the Hamlets I have seen, the actors, and the entertainment was in the many ways to do it, to interpret it. It stimulates my thoughts and I am absorbed by it. That is entertainment.

When people make these silly remarks about messages being sent by Western Union, they reveal their own foolishness and superficiality. An obvious message is not entertaining, it is bad and silly; but if we teach people while getting them to listen, and they go away with something to discuss with their friends, that is more entertaining than just laughing. The word "entertaining" is a dangerous word because people interpret it as being "to make you laugh, and feel good." We don't need films to do this. Just drink enough, get somebody to tickle you, and laugh!

Filmography—Second Period

THE MOON IS BLUE. 1953. *Director:* Otto Preminger. *Screenplay:* F. Hugh Herbert. *Based on his play "The Moon Is Blue." Photography:* Ernest Laszlo. *Production Designer:* Nicolai Remisoff. *Set Director:* Edward G. Boyle. *Editors:* Louis R. Loeffler, Otto Ludwig. *Music:* Herschel Burke Gilbert. *Lyrics:* Sylvia Fine. *Wardrobe Designer:* Don Loper. *Producers:* Otto Preminger and F. Hugh Herbert. *Release:* United Artists, June 3, 1953. 99 mins. *Players:* Maggie McNamara (*Patty O'Neill*),

William Holden with Maggie McNamara in THE MOON IS BLUE

William Holden (*Don Gresham*), David Niven (*David Slater*), Dawn Addams (*Cynthia Slater*), Gregory Ratoff (*Taxi Driver*), Fortunio Bonanova (*Television Announcer*), Hardy Krüger and Johanna Matz (*A couple in the final scene*).

At the same time, using the same crew of technicians, a German version of the play was also filmed: DIE JUNGFRAU AUF DEM DACH. *Dialogue:* Carl Zuckmayer. Players as above, except: Hardy Krüger (*Don Gresham*), Johanna Matz (*Patty O'Neill*), Johannes Heesters (*David Slater*). Gregory Ratoff was dubbed by Otto Preminger.

Story

Don Gresham, a successful architect, engages a young actress, Patty O'Neill, in conversation on top of the Empire State Building, and she accepts his invitation to dinner. Dropping in at his apartment on the way, they decide to dine there as Patty announces herself an excellent cook. Don slips out to buy food, and Patty is briefly visited by his ex-fiancée, Cynthia, and not so briefly, by Cynthia's father David, a middle-aged, practised charmer who, on her invitation, stays to dinner. A slight accident at the table occasions Patty to change her dress for Don's dressing-

gown. *While Don is away placating the jealous Cynthia, David loses no time in offering Patty a proposal of marriage and a six hundred dollar gift. She accepts the latter and is surprised by Don in a grateful kiss to David. Don is still enraged with Patty when her father arrives, and, outraged to discover his daughter in a bachelor's apartment, knocks him senseless. Later David returns, interrupts a reconciliation, and also misinterprets the situation. The misunderstandings are cleared up the next day when, simultaneously drawn to the Empire State Building, Patty accepts Don's proposal of marriage.*

Preminger: See page 100.

RIVER OF NO RETURN. 1954. *Director:* Otto Preminger. *Screenplay:* Frank Fenton. *Based on a story by:* Louis Lantz. *Photography* (CinemaScope, Technicolor): Joseph La Shelle. *Art Directors:* Lyle Wheeler, Addison Hehr. *Set Directors:* Walter M. Scott, Chester Bayhi. *Special Effects:* Ray Kellogg. *Editor:* Louis Loeffler. *Music:* Cyril Mockridge. *Musical Director:* Lionel Newman *with orchestration by:* Edward Powell. *Songs:* "River of No Return," "One Silver Dollar," "I'm Going to File My Claim," "Down in the Meadow." *Music:* Lionel Newman. *Lyrics:* Ken Darby. *Technicolor Adviser:* Leonard Doss. *Choreography:* Jack Cole. *Wardrobe Designers:* Charles Le Maire, Travilla. *Producer:* Stanley Rubin. *Release:* 20th. Century-Fox, April 23, 1954. 91 mins. *Players:* Robert Mitchum (*Matt Calder*), Marilyn Monroe (*Kay Weston*), Rory Calhoun (*Harry Weston*), Tommy Rettig (*Mark Calder*), Murvyn Vye (*Dave Colby*), Douglas Spencer (*Sam Benson*), Ed Winton (*A Gambler*), Don Beddoe (*Ben*), Claire André (*Surrey Driver*), Jack Mather (*A Croupier*), Edmund Cobb (*A Barber*), Will Wright (*Merchant*), Jarma Lewis (*Dancer*), Hal Baylor (*A Drunken Cowboy*), Arthur Shields (*The Minister*), John Doucette (*Spectator in the Black Nugget*).

Story

During the Gold Rush of 1875, a widower, Matt Calder, is released from prison after serving a sentence for shooting a man in the back. With his ten-year-old son who knows nothing of his father's past, he plans to develop his farm, which borders on the River of No Return.

One morning they see a raft out of control, and rescue from it Kay, a saloon singer, and Harry Weston, her gambler husband. They are hurrying to Council City to register a gold claim won by Harry in a card game. Matt tells them that they will never make it by river, and, after a fight, Harry takes his gun and his only horse and goes off alone, leaving Kay to look after the injured Matt.

Soon afterwards, Indians attack the farm and all three escape by raft. Matt is determined, if they stay alive, to bring Harry to justice; and in between fighting off Indians and negotiating the rapids, Kay tries to persuade him to change his mind. At one camp-site she loses her temper and tells Matt that she knows about his past. Mark overhears and refuses to listen to Matt's explanation that he had to shoot to save a friend's life. Two camp-sites later, Kay apologises: she has come to respect Matt's attitude to life.

When at last they reach Council City, Kay finds Harry, unrepentant, gambling in the saloon. She begs him to face Matt and apologise. Harry agrees, but treacherously pulls out his gun. Before he can fire, Mark shoots him in the back. Father and son are reconciled; later, they collect Kay and return to re-build the farm.

Preminger: This was one of the films I owed Zanuck under my contract. Like *The Thirteenth Letter* it was filmed in part in Canada, and I remember little of it. I liked the script, and I was interested in using the new lenses called CinemaScope. It is actually more difficult to compose in this size; also in Panavision. Few painters have chosen these proportions, and somehow it embraces more, we see more widely, and it fits into long takes better. On the wide screen, abrupt cuts disturb audiences. I don't

Robert Mitchum with Marilyn Monroe in THE RIVER OF NO RETURN

believe in cutting too much or doing too many reaction shots.

CARMEN JONES. 1954. *Director:* Otto Preminger. *Screenplay:* Harry Kleiner. *Based on a musical comedy by:* Oscar Hammerstein II (taken from a comic opera by Meilhac and Halévy, based on a novel by Mérimée and produced on Broadway by Billie Rose). *Photography* (CinemaScope, Colour by De Luxe): Sam Leavitt and Albert Myers. *Art Director:* Edward L. Ilou. *Set Director:* Claude E. Carpenter. *Editor:* Louis R. Loeffler. *Sound:* Roger Heman, Arthur L. Kirbach. *Music:* Herschel Burke Gilbert based on the music of Georges

Dorothy Dandridge with Harry Belafonte in CARMEN JONES

Bizet. *Choreography*: Herbett Ross. *Fight Scenes*: John Indrisano. *Wardrobe Designer*: Mary Ann Nyberg. *Titles*: Saul Bass. *Producer*: Otto Preminger. *Production*: Carlyle Production. *Release*: 20th. Century-Fox, October 5, 1954. 107 mins. *Players*: Dorothy Dandridge (*Carmen Jones*), Harry Belafonte (*Joe*), Olga James (*Cindy Lou*), Pearl Bailey (*Frankie*), Diahann Carroll (*Myrt*), Roy Glenn (*Rum*), Nick Stewart (*Dink*), Joe Adams (*Husky Miller*), Brock Peters (*Sgt. Brown*), Sandy Lewis (*T-Bone*), Maurie Lynn (*Sally*), DeForest Covan (*Entertainer*), Rubin Wilson (*Husky's Opponent*), Carmen De Lavallade and Archie Savage (*Dance Soloists*).

Singing Voices: Le Vern Hutcherson (*Joe*), Marilynn Horne (*Carmen*), Marvin Hayes (*Husky*), Bernice Patterson (*Myrt*), Brock Peters (*Rum*), Joe Crawford (*Dink*).

Story

Cindy Lou visits a parachute factory near Jacksonville to say good-bye to her fiancé, Joe, off to flying school to train as a pilot, and discovers that Carmen Jones, one of the factory girls, is after him. Joe is obliged to escort Carmen to Masonville jail after she has become involved in a fight; she persuades him to let her stop at her grandmother's house on the way, and seduces him there. Then she escapes and Joe is sent to prison for negligence. Carmen, though offered a trip to Chicago by a boxer, decides to wait for Joe.

When he comes out of jail they are reunited; she persuades him not to go back to flying school, but to come with her to Chicago. The lovers hide out in a tenement room and soon Carmen is bored and penniless. They quarrel, and Carmen finds solace with the boxer. Joe, desperate and jealous, strangles her and waits for arrest by the Military Police.

Preminger: This was really a fantasy, as was *Porgy and Bess*. The all-black world shown in these films doesn't exist, at least not in the United States. We used the musical-fantasy quality to convey something of the needs and aspirations of coloured people. Later, I moved into an objective reality with *Hurry Sundown*.

THE MAN WITH THE GOLDEN ARM.

1955. *Director :* Otto Preminger. *Screenplay :* Walter Newman, Lewis Meltzer. *Based on the novel by :* Nelson Algren. *Photography :* Sam Leavitt. *Art Director :* Joe Wright. *Set Director :* Darrell Silvera. *Editor :* Louis R. Loeffler. *Sound :* Jack Solomon. *Music :* Elmer Bernstein. *Wardrobe Designers :* Joe King (men), Adele Parmenter (women), Mary Ann Nyberg (supervision). *Titles :* Saul Bass. *Producer :* Otto Preminger. *Production :* Carlyle Production. *Release :* United Artists, December 14, 1955. 119 mins. *Players :* Frank Sinatra (*Frankie Machine*), Kim Novak (*Molly*), Eleanor Parker (*Zosch*), Arnold Stang (*Sparrow*), Darren McGavin (*Louis*), Robert Strauss (*Schwiefka*), George Matthews (*Williams*), John Conte (*Drunky*), Doro Merande (*Vi*), George E. Stone (*Sam Markette*), Emil Meyer (*Inspector Bednar*), Himself (*Shorty Rogers*), Himself (*Shelly Manne*), Leonid Kinskey (*Dr. Dominowski*), Frank Richards (*Piggy*), Ralph Neff (*Chester*), Ernest Raboff (*Bird-Dog*), Marth Wentworth (*Vaugie*), Jerry Barclay (*Junkie*), Leonard Bremen (*Taxi Driver*), Paul Burns (*Suspenders*), Charles Seel (*Proprie-*

Kim Novak with Frank Sinatra in THE MAN WITH THE GOLDEN ARM

tor), Will Wright (*Lane*), Tommy Hart (*Kvorka*), Frank Marlowe (*Antek*), Joe McTurk (*Meter Reader*).

Story

Frankie, a drug addict, returns to the Chicago slums after a jail sentence. He has been cured of his addiction, has discovered an unsuspected talent as a drummer, and is determined to give up his former life. But pressure from his wife, Zosch, a neurotic cripple in a wheelchair, from his ex-employer Schwiefka, and from Louis (a dope pedlar), drives him back to his old occupation as a poker dealer, and eventually, to drugs.

Encouraged by Molly, his faithful girl friend, Frankie makes a final effort

*to break free and arranges an audition
with a band. But he agrees to play one
last game for Schwiefka, an exhausting
two-day poker session which wrecks his
chances at the audition. He quarrels
violently with Louis when refused a
further shot of dope, and comes under
suspicion when Louis is later found
dead. In fact the killer is Zosch, whose
lameness is merely a hysterical pretence
to keep Frankie, and who has been
found out by Louis. Frankie hides in
Molly's room and there undergoes a
violent cure. Zosch, her guilt discovered,
hurls herself to her death. Frankie and
Molly are left to build their lives together.*

Preminger: The film, as everybody
knows by now, encountered objec-
tions in different circles, particularly
from the Motion Pictures Producers'
Association of America, which usually
gives its Seal of approval to films. It
refused the Seal for this picture, because its Code says that dope addiction and the illegal traffic in narcotics
must never be presented in films.
Well, naturally, I knew this when I
started the picture, but I imagined
that if the film met with certain standards, they would either amend the
Code or grant this film an exception.
I don't, by the way, care too much
whether the picture gets the Seal or
not, because the Seal is completely
out-moded since the theatres and the
production of pictures have been
divorced by the government in an
anti-trust suit. The Seal has no
power. The surprising thing is that I
felt I had made a picture which has
what I would call a very strong moral
lesson, or a moral balance at least. I
don't feel that I made a picture which
in any way could induce people to
take narcotics. On the contrary, I feel
that if anything this picture is a warning against the consequence of taking
narcotics. Therefore I was surprised
that the M.P.P.A. did not change its
point of view; but on the other hand it
is not that surprising, because it acted
on a basis of bureaucracy, of pedantic
interpretation of a Code which was
written thirty years ago, so what can
you expect? Anyway, I don't want to
talk about this too much. I was very
gratified with the reception the picture received yesterday, the first public showing at the Victoria Theatre in
New York, and my only judge when I
make pictures is the public. I don't
believe that a film-maker can know
beforehand what an audience is going
to accept, or is bound to like. I can
only work by doing something that
satisfies my own interests. In other
words, I selected this picture for no
reason other than I had read and re-
read it over several years, and I always
wanted to put these particular characters, which fascinated me, on the
screen, and I finally did. I am also
interested, at the same time, in the

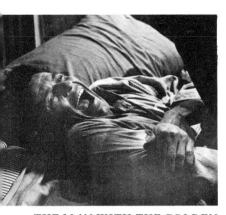

THE MAN WITH THE GOLDEN ARM : Frank Sinatra "going cold turkey"

national problem of narcotics. However, this was secondary. I only started to study drugs after I'd read the novel, and the picture hasn't even one-tenth of what could be explosive and dramatic material on this subject. I do think that if this picture is followed by others it can only do good; exposing a sore is much better than hiding it. To claim we have no narcotics problem in this country, to say that the youngsters are not being induced by dope pedlars to take dope, is foolish.

I've heard in discussing the film with some critics that they would have liked to see more of the reasons why the man, in the first place, became addicted to narcotics. If you study the question, you will find there are many reasons for starting to take dope. Some people start by having an operation, being given it by doctors and then get used to it. One of the most usual excuses is that people started in the war. I deliberately didn't use any of these, because I felt that it was much more realistic to show (and he tells it in the picture in a big scene, if you remember) that he just took it for fun at first, and this is the most dangerous reason. If people take it for "kicks," as they call it, and they think, as he says in the picture, "I thought I could take it or leave it, and suddenly I noticed I couldn't leave it any more," there is the danger: that we all feel we are exceptions in these matters, we can just try it, and then let it go. This is the danger with alcohol, with narcotics, with all kinds of things—that we feel we are stronger than other people. I also tried to show in the picture, that the psychological cause is really what keeps the man on narcotics. The physical cure is comparatively easy today, if you take it in the hospital with the help of drugs and doctors. But the psychological cure is very hard. Statistics show that people fall back into the habit in alarmingly high numbers, because of mental unhappiness. Maybe it starts with the pace of the life we live, with mature people taking sleeping pills and benzedrine. Then they go to more harmful poison.

I say what I like because it is completely my picture, an independent picture. I am the producer, the director, the casting director, it's all my decision. As a matter of fact, even the publicity and the advertisements are determined by me, which makes it great fun to do a picture, because I used to work in major studios, where many of these things were taken out of your hands. I don't think it's a good system. Now it is changing. I think many directors control their pictures because the major studio set-up is very shaky. The major studios make very few really successful pictures these days. They really exist on the fact that they have also distribution and other sidelines to make money. In the present market, every picture must be an individual enterprise, it has to show a kind of showmanship and a special treatment that make people come to see it. Mass production is something which doesn't work today any more, and that makes the situation of the major studios very difficult. In discussing economics, the strange paradoxical thing about pictures is that in any other field of business or industry (that's why I hate when people call movies an industry) mass production is always

much cheaper. If you tried to produce a Ford car, it would probably cost you five thousand times the money that it costs Ford to do that, but if you do a picture independently, it costs you much less than if M-G-M or Fox do the same picture.

CBC, New York, April 1956

THE COURT MARTIAL OF BILLY MITCHELL (British title: **ONE MAN MUTINY**). 1955. *Director :* Otto Preminger. *Screenplay :* Milton Sperling and Emmet Lavery. *Based on a true story by :* Gen. William Mitchell. *Photography* (CinemaScope, Warnercolor): Sam Leavitt. *Art Director :* Malcolm Bert. *Set Director :* William Kuehl. *Special Effects :* H. F. Koenenkamp. *Editor :* Folmar Blangsted. *Music :* Dimitri Tiomkin. *Wardrobe Designer :* Howard Shoup. *Second Unit :* Russ Saunders. *Technical Adviser :* Maj.-Gen. Douglas Keeney. *Producer :* Milton Sperling. *Production :* United States Production. *Release :* Warner Brothers, December 31, 1955. 100 mins. *Players :* Gary Cooper (*Brig.-Gen. William Mitchell*), Charles Bickford (*Gen. James Guthrie*), Rod Steiger (*Maj. Allen Gullion*), Ralph Bellamy (*Congressman Frank Reid*), Elizabeth Montgomery (*Margaret Lansdowne*), Fred Clark (*Col. Moreland*), James Daly (*Col. Herbert A. White*), Darren McGavin (*Russ

Peters), Jack Lord (*Zachary Lansdowne*), Peter Graves (*Captain Elliott*), Robert F. Simon (*Admiral Adam Gage*), Charles Dingle (*Senator Fullerton*), Dayton Lummis (*Gen. Douglas MacArthur*), Tom McKee (*Capt. Eddie Rickenbacker*), Steve Roberts (*Maj. Carl Spaatz*), Herbert Heyes (*Gen. John Pershing*), Robert Brubaker (*Maj. H. H. Arnold*), Phil Arnold (*Fiorello La Guardia*), Ian Wolfe (*President Calvin Coolidge*), Will Wright (*Admiral William S. Sims*), John Maxwell, Stuart Holmes (*Members of the jury*), Steve Holland (*Stu Stuart*), Adam Kennedy (*Yip Ryan*), Manning Ross (*Ted Adams*), Carleton Young (*Gen. Pershing's Aide-de-Camp*), Robert B. Williams (*Carl Tuttle*).

Gary Cooper (centre) in THE COURT MARTIAL OF BILLY MITCHELL

Story

After the First World War, Brig.-General Billy Mitchell, Assistant Chief of the Army Air Service, wishes to impress upon the War Department the importance of air power in defence and attack. He persuades Army and Navy to allow him to try to sink, with aerial bombs, the former "unsinkable" German battleship "Ostfriesland." They impose conditions regarding the bombing altitude and the weight of the bombs used. The first test fails, and it is by employing heavier bombs and flying at a lower level that Mitchell successfully sinks the battleship at a second attempt.

For disobeying orders, he is relieved of his command and reduced in rank.

After a long letter-writing campaign, stressing the inadequacy of America's air power and following a series of air disasters, he makes a press statement accusing the War Department of "incompetence and criminal negligence." He is immediately arrested and ordered to face court martial. Mitchell pleads "Not Guilty," hoping to prolong the trial and thus create public interest. After an exhausting trial, he is finally found guilty and dismissed from the service. But with public reaction high, he is confident that, al-

though his own career has been sacrificed, the administrative reforms for which he has fought, will now come.

Preminger: This is another of my independent films when I was not entirely independent and had a producer. This was not a film initiated by me. I was asked to do it and as usual when it is not my production, I had producer difficulties, this time with Milton Sperling.

The producer of this film is actually a very nice and intelligent man, but he seemed to have a tremendous inferiority complex. Whenever he suggested something, and we liked it and incorporated it in the script, he came back the next day and changed it again. This went on until neither Ben Hecht nor I had the patience to go through with it. He was the only man I ever saw Gary Cooper get angry at. Because he had this strange negative quality.

SAINT JOAN. 1957. *Director:* Otto Preminger. *Screenplay:* Graham Greene. *Based on the play* "Saint Joan" *by:* Bernard Shaw. *Photography:* Georges Périnal. *Production Designer:* Roger Furse. *Art Director:* Raymond Simm. *Editor:* Helga Cranston. *Sound:* Peter Hanford, Red Law. *Music:* Mischa Spolianski. *Historical Consultant:* Dr. Charles Beard. *Titles:* Saul Bass. *Producer:* Otto

Richard Todd and Jean Seberg in SAINT JOAN

Preminger. *Production:* Preminger Productions. *Release:* United Artists, May 8, 1957. 110 mins. (Filmed in England.) *Players:* Jean Seberg (*Saint Joan*), Richard Widmark (*Charles, The Dauphin*), Richard Todd (*Dunois*), Anton Walbrook (*Cauchon, Bishop of Beauvais*), John Gielgud (*Earl of Warwick*), Felix Aylmer (*The Inquisitor*), Harry Andrews (*John de Stogumber*), Barry Jones (*de Courcelles*), Finlay Currie (*Archbishop of Rheims*), Bernard Miles (*The Executioner*), Patrick Barr (*Captain La Hire*), Kenneth Haigh (*Brother Martin*), Archie Duncan (*Baudricourt*), Margot Grahame (*Duchess of la Trémouille*), Francis de Wolfe

(*La Trémouille*), Victor Maddern (*An English soldier*), David Oxley (*Gilles de Rais, "Bluebeard"*), Sidney Bromley (*Baudricourt's steward*), David Langton (*Captain of Warwick's Guard*).

Story

Joan, a simple French farm girl, arrives at the Dauphin's palace of Chinon with a letter from Captain de Baudricourt. After some argument the Dauphin makes Joan a Commander of his Army. Her first battle against the English, at Orléans, is a victory for the French, and the Dauphin is crowned King. Against the wishes of the new King and his court, Joan goes on to Paris to fight the English. At Compiègne, she is captured by the Burgundians and later sold to the English Commander, the Earl of Warwick.

Turned over to the church to be tried, she undergoes nine months of imprisonment and questioning, and finally comes to trial at Rouen. Threatened with torture, Joan signs a confession of heresy; but when she learns that her sentence is to be one of life long solitary imprisonment, she tears up her confession. Warwick, tired of the continual bickering of the church, orders Joan's immediate execution. At the stake, Joan is burned to death as a heretic.

Preminger: I have for a long time been wanting to put Bernard Shaw's play, *Saint Joan*, which I consider one of the greatest plays ever written, on the screen. Finally, after two years of negotiations, I acquired the rights and I want to offer the part of Joan, a very well written part indeed, to an unknown actress, to a new face for the movies, and if possible, if she's successful, it will be what you kindly called her, "a new star." We started this search a couple of months ago in the movie theatres by having a trailer, which I filmed, explain the conditions for the search, and by distributing application blanks. We received about eighteen thousand applications in my Hollywood office which were weeded down to three thousand. I am going to see three thousand girls on this tour which I started last week in New York and which will lead me to fifteen cities in the United States, two cities in Canada, four cities in Britain, starting in London and going to Dublin, Glasgow and Manchester and then Stockholm where people learn English in school. Language is a problem, of course. I think it would not be objectionable if the girl who actually was French, would have a slight accent, but she would have to be able to be in complete control of the English language in order to play this part. All over the world, United Artists' branch managers are watching for me and if they find somebody, they might send them down, either to London or to New York where I am

SAINT JOAN : Jean Seberg goes to the stake

going to make final tests and then announcing on a national television show on October 21 the winner. I'm starting rehearsals actually in the second part of December, and on January 2, I am starting to shoot in London. I am planning to have an all-star cast, around an unknown actress, or until now an unknown actress, and I have signed definitely only one actor, Richard Widmark, and he's going to play the Dauphin, which is quite a change from his usual parts. He's very enthusiastic about it. I met him in New York last week when I arrived from London and he made a deal, and I am negotiating with some other actors, quite well-known, but I hate to announce anything until it is definite, because it leads to confusion. I am making the film in England because most of the small parts are character parts, which I can cast better there.

I have no specific image or character in mind. I only know there are certain qualities necessary to portray this part, which I hope to recognise when I meet the girl. There is a great deal of sincerity, honesty, an almost fanatic devotion which this girl must be able to portray or to personify, and naturally, also talent. There is a great misunderstanding when people think I am looking for an unknown actress who never acted. I mean she could have acted in the theatre, on television, even played smaller parts in the movies. I'm only using the word "unknown" in contrast to a very well-established star, not that an established star couldn't play it, but the idea is that this whole project might gain in excitement and interest if I am able to bring a new personality to play this part.

There is now in New York a production of Shaw's *Saint Joan* with Siobhan McKenna which I saw in Philadelphia, and I liked her very much. It was a very moving, very good performance, and she uses, by the way, an Irish brogue in portraying the girl. I think she has many of the qualities I want in my St. Joan, but I don't know if she's a movie actress.

Maybe eventually, if she's interested, I would like to make a test, but she's never been in movies and, as you know, there is a great deal of difference between stage and screen actors. Many of our greatest actresses, just because they are great actresses, never succeeded in movies. The movies are looking for a "being" . . . the greatest actresses developed a certain style and nothing that is very stylised has ever succeeded in movies. That's why many of our movie stars, who have great success and give very good performances in the movies, could never work on the stage. They are not really good actresses in the stage sense. These are two different mediums. There's also another question which is very important. It's easier, comparatively, for an actress from the stage to project youth—and this role needs youth, because St. Joan was seventeen when she was burned at the stake, and while I don't think it must be an actress of seventeen, she ought to be near to it. On the stage the audience accepts an older actress. The part was originally played by Sybil Thorndike when she was forty-one and she made a big success, but the camera is much more discerning, we have to be more authentic, it comes closer, and the public is less sophisticated. They don't forgive.

I do not talk about my budget. I think altogether too much is being said about money being spent on pictures, and their costs. My pictures cost $2.00 or $2.50 or however much you pay at theatres to see my film! I think some subjects should be done as spectacular pictures and some don't need it, and should not be unnecessarily extended or expanded, because they only become dull. No picture is particularly good because it is on a wide screen, and has colour and has a lot of extras in it, because extras in themselves are not very interesting, but some pictures need them. Some stories need to be told this way, like let's say *The Ten Commandments* or *The King and I*, but I am doing this *Saint Joan* picture deliberately in black-and-white, on the normal screen, because I want to put the emphasis on people, on characterisations, on emotions, and on the words by Bernard Shaw. I am not just doing another St. Joan, another story of Joan of Arc. I am doing Bernard Shaw's *Saint Joan*, a very successful play in 1923, which I think should be shown as he wrote it. Colour, or too much spectacle added to it, would distract rather than help to give this play to the public. We are filming the play a little differently, but we are not adding any battle scenes. Graham Greene is writing the screenplay, we are strictly adhering to the Shaw dialogue, but we are telling the story

in a little different continuity, in order to adjust it, adapt it to the picture medium.

CBC, Toronto, September 9, 1956

BONJOUR TRISTESSE. 1957. *Director:* Otto Preminger. *Screenplay:* Arthur Laurents. *Based on the novel by:* Françoise Sagan. *Photography* (CinemaScope, Technicolor): Georges Périnal. *Production Designer:* Roger Furse. *Art Director:* Raymond Simm. *Set Director:* Georges Petitot. *Editor:* Helga Cranston. *Sound Editor:* David Hawkins. *Sound:* David Hildyard, Red Law. *Assistant Directors:* Adrian Pryce-Jones, Serge Friedman. *Music:* Georges Auric. *Conductor:* Lambert Williamson. *Camera Operator:* Denys Coop. *Dances:* Tutte Lemkow. *Costume Co-ordination:* Hope Bryce. *Gowns:* Givenchy. *Jewellery:* Cartiers. *Accessories:* Hermes. *Wardrobe:* May Walding. *Make-up:* George Frost. *Hairstyles:* Gordon Bond, Janou Pottier. *Script Supervisor:* Eileen Head. *Paintings:* Kumi Sagai. *Cast and Credits:* Saul Bass. *Producer:* Otto Preminger. *Associate Producer:* John Palmer. *Assistant to the Producer:* Maximilian Slater. *Production Managers:* Erica Masters,

At left: Jean Seberg with Geoffrey Horne in BONJOUR TRISTESSE

Philippe Senne. *Production:* Wheel Films. *Release:* Columbia, January 16, 1958. 93 mins. (Filmed in France.) *Players:* Deborah Kerr (*Anne Larsen*), David Niven (*Raymond*), Jean Seberg (*Cécile*), Mylène Demongeot (*Elsa Mackenbourg*), Geoffrey Horne (*Philippe*), Juliette Greco (*Night club singer*), Walter Chiari (*Pablo*), Martita Hunt (*Philippe's Mother*), Roland Culver (*Mr. Lombard*), Jean Kent (*Mrs. Lombard*), David Oxley (*Jacques*), Elga Anderson (*Denise*), Jeremy Burnham (*Hubert Duclos*), Eveline Eyfel (*The Maid*), Tutte Lemkow (*Pierre Schube*).

Story

A wealthy Parisian widower, Raymond, and his teenage daughter, Cécile, live a life of uninterrupted pleasure. Thoroughly spoiled and pampered, Cécile readily forgives her father's romantic escapades. When they take a villa in the south of France with Elsa, Raymond's latest mistress, Cécile is immediately attracted to Philippe, the son of a wealthy neighbour. Elsa is ousted by an attractive widow, Anne, Cécile's godmother, who comes to stay for a short visit at the villa; Raymond, unable to seduce her, has to propose. As Raymond's fiancée, Anne is in a position to criticise Cécile's behaviour;

At right: Deborah Kerr with David Niven in BONJOUR TRISTESSE

the criticism is fiercely resented and Cécile plots with Philippe to reinstate Elsa with her father. The plan works, and Anne, distraught with grief, drives recklessly away from the villa. Her car crashes and she is killed. Both father and daughter realise that they are responsible for her death; when they return to Paris the round of night clubs and cocktail parties begins again; but the pleasures are hollow and their old care-free existence is lost for ever.

Preminger: *Bonjour Tristesse* is a film I like. I rarely say this, but I really don't think the American critics did it justice. You know, it was a very big success in France, and in America the critics said it wasn't French enough, which is very funny.

PORGY AND BESS. 1959. *Director:* Otto Preminger. *Screenplay:* Richard Nash. *Based on the stage operetta by:* George Gershwin *from the novel* "Porgy" *by:* Dubose and Dorothy Heyward.* *Photography* (Todd-AO, Technicolor): Leon Shamroy. *Production Designer:* Oliver Smith. *Art Directors:* Serge Krizman, Joseph Wright. *Set Director:* Howard Bristol. *Editor:* Daniel Mandell. *Sound:* Gordon Sawyer, Fred Hynes. Stereophonic. *Music:* George Gershwin. *Musical Director:* André Previn. *Associate Musical Director:* Ken Darby. *Choreography:* Hermes Pan. *Wardrobe Designer:* Irene Sharaff.

Producer: Samuel Goldwyn. *Production:* A Samuel Goldwyn Production. *Release:* Columbia, June 25, 1959. 146 mins plus intermission. *Players:* Sidney Poitier (*Porgy*), Dorothy Dandridge (*Bess*), Sammy Davis Jr. (*Sportin' Life*), Pearl Bailey (*Maria*), Brock Peters (*Crown*), Leslie Scott (*Jake*), Diahann Carroll (*Clara*), Ruth Attaway (*Serena*), Clarence Muse (*Peter*), Everdinne Wilson (*Annie*), Joel Fluellen (*Robbins*), Earl Jackson (*Mingo*), Moses LaMarr (*Nelson*), Margaret Hairston (*Lily*), Ivan Dixon (*Jim*), Antoine Durousseau (*Scipio*), Helen Thigpen (*Strawberry Woman*), Vince Townsend Jr. (*Elderly Man*), Roy Glenn (*Lawyer Frazier*), William Walker (*Undertaker*), Claude Akins (*Detective*), Maurice Manson (*Coroner*).

Principal Singing Voices: Robert McFerrin (*Porgy*), Adele Addison (*Bess*), Sammy Davis Jr. (*Sportin' Life*), Pearl Bailey (*Maria*), Brock Peters (*Crown*), Loulie Jean Norman (*Clara*), Inez Matthews (*Serena*).

The Songs: *Music by:* George Gershwin. *Lyrics by:* Dubose Heyward and Ira Gershwin. "Summertime," "A Woman is a Sometime Thing," "Honey Man's Call," "They Pass by Singing," "Oh Little Stars," "Gone, Gone, Gone," "Fill Up De Saucer," "My Man's Gone Now," "The Train Is at the Station," "Oh, I Got Plenty O' Nuttin'," "Bess, You Is My

Woman Now," "Oh, I Can't Sit Down," "I Ain't Got No Shame," "It Ain't Necessarily So," "What You Want Wid Bess," "It Takes a Long Pull To Get There," "Strawberry Woman's Call," "Crab Man's Call," "I Loves You Porgy," "Oh, De Lawd Shake de Heaven," "Dere's Somebody Knockin' at de Do'," "A Red Headed Woman," "Clara, Don't You Be Downhearted," "There's a Boat Dat's Leavin' Soon for New York," "Good mornin', Sistuh," "Oh, Where's My Bess?" "Oh, Lawd, I'm on My Way."

* *The Background:* Dubose Heyward's *Porgy* first appeared as a novel in 1925. Two years later, he and his wife, Dorothy, completed their stage adaptation and the play opened on Broadway, October 10, 1927. The Theatre Guild produced, Rouben Mamoulian directed, Frank Wilson was Porgy and Evelyn Ellis was Bess. Meanwhile, George Gershwin was interested in transforming the play into what he termed a "Folk Opera." Eight years later, he finished the score, with lyrics by his brother Ira, and the first production of *Porgy and Bess* took place in Boston. It opened on Broadway at the Majestic Theatre on October 11, 1935. The Theatre Guild again produced, Mamoulian again directed, and Todd Duncan was Porgy and Anne Brown was Bess. It was only a moderate success,

PORGY AND BESS: Poitier, Dandridge, and Sammy Davis Jr. at left

chalking up one hundred and twenty-four performances. Only after Gershwin's death did *Porgy and Bess* achieve current fame. Cheryl Crawford revived it in 1942, retained most of the 1935 principals but changed the musical recitative to spoken dialogue, and the production was an enormous success. The film version was to have been directed by Mamoulian, but after a disagreement with Goldwyn he left and Preminger took over.

Story

When Crown, a huge bully, kills a man in a street fight, his girl Bess seeks shelter from the police in the shack of a crippled beggar, Porgy. Although a loose woman, much resented by the other

women of Catfish Row, with Porgy she
finds real love for the first time in her
life. She rejects the offers of the dope-
pedlar Sportin' Life to take her away to
New York, and by staying on with
Porgy she begins to gain respect from the
people around her.

On the day of the annual picnic she
reluctantly leaves Porgy to join the
others on Kittiwah Island; she is
attacked and held there by Crown who
has been hiding from the police. After
three days he sends her back hysterical,
warning her that he will soon come and
claim her for good.

When Crown arrives, Porgy manages
to kill him in a fight; when the police
arrive, although Porgy is not suspected,
he is taken away to identify the body.
Seizing his opportunity, Sportin' Life
now moves in on Bess and by assuring
her that Porgy will never be set free,
succeeds in persuading her to go to New
York with him.

Porgy returns and, finding Bess gone,
sets off in search of her and of his lost
happiness. His friends then gather at
the entrance of the courtyard and wish
him luck as he sets out on his way.

Preminger: Samuel Goldwyn is a
man who undoubtedly had his day,
and had his virtues as a businessman,
a producer who always tried to get the

Opposite : Sidney Poitier and Dorothy
Dandridge in PORGY AND BESS

most out of his money. He came to
me one day after he had seen the
rushes for *Porgy and Bess* (I hadn't
seen them yet) and said: "The rushes
are wonderful, they are beautifully
photographed." I said to him: "Why
don't you tell Shamroy," the cameraman, who was standing four feet
away. He replied: "Why should I tell
him! I pay him enough!" That was
his attitude. He always felt he paid
people when he wanted to get something out of them. It was fine for him
and it probably made him, but he was
always Goldwyn. Few people have
respect for a man like him, and I certainly didn't have respect for him. He
didn't contribute one useful thought,
or word of advice throughout the
entire production. He knew so little
that he came to the stage another time,
after he had seen the rushes, and
said: "A beautiful day but a little
dark. Don't you think for the smaller
version you should have more light?"
I said "What smaller version?" We
had been shooting two weeks in 70
mm, and he said: "Well, the 35 mm
version." "But, Sam," I said, "we
only shoot one version, and if you
want it in 35 mm it will be optically
reduced"—which everybody knows.
He didn't believe me. "You are
putting me on! You are kidding!" I
told him this was the procedure. He
went from one person to another to
see if I had been lying. The producer,

after several weeks of shooting, did not know that we shot only one version and the reducing was done optically. He never knew much. He had a very good business brain. He tried to get the most out of his money and he tested people to see if they really knew their business, even when they had proved themselves. He had a function, but he was not a producer like David Selznick or Zanuck, who really inspired people, and contributed something. He only knew always to buy the best. He bought William Wyler, he bought the best writers and actors, when they were in the market, or tried to buy them for the cheapest money. Billy Wilder, on the first day I started shooting (he was on the same lot) said: "Look out for you. We know this is going to be Sam Goldwyn's last picture. Don't make it yours too." I remember I was out on location and he phoned me, and said the shots didn't match, or something. I flew in and they matched beautifully. He only wanted to see if we knew our business, he had an awful way of testing people, a cold-blooded, very egotistical man, always afraid of people. I remember on that occasion we came to his house, it was Sunday, and we looked at the rushes there. He had a beautiful painting by Picasso, and as we left the cameraman stopped and said: "This is a beautiful picture, Mr. Goldwyn." He said: "This

painting belongs to my wife!" He was afraid the cameraman would expect him to give it to him!

I directed the film for him because he had trouble with Mamoulian. He remembered the time Mamoulian was supposed to do *Laura*, and didn't, and he reasoned "if Preminger directed *Laura* instead of Mamoulian, he will also do a good job directing *Porgy and Bess*." I was free, he called me and with my brother (who was an agent at that time and represented me) we made a contract. It was very funny, by the way. My brother discussed with him the terms, a profit participation, apart from the salary, and he offered my brother a ten per cent profit participation. My brother said: "This is ridiculous, it is not enough." He called me, I wanted to do the film and I said: "Tell Mr. Goldwyn that when the picture is finished, we leave it to him. When the picture is finished he will determine the profit participation," thinking that the least I can get would be the ten per cent he offered me now. The picture was finished, and we didn't talk much any more, and my brother went in and said: "Well, Mr. Goldwyn, what about the profit participation. You must decide it now." He said: "What profit participation?" My brother replied: "But don't you remember we couldn't get together, and my brother said he leaves the profit participation to you?" Goldwyn answered "He leaves the profit participation to me? No profit participation!" So he didn't give me anything, I didn't get any profit participation.

I always believe money is something which, if you work hard enough, you make enough. When you are very rich, like Howard Hughes, you can use money as a weapon. I like money only to be able to live well, to enjoy my surroundings, give my children an education, to leave enough money when I die so that my children and wife can live well enough in the same way, my children can be educated and make their own way in life. I don't want to be the richest man when I die, it doesn't mean that much to me. I think that's the last time I worked with a producer. As for Mamoulian, I am not his keeper. A book about him claims that I used footage in *Laura* which was shot by him, which is not true. Not one shot of what he did in *Laura* was kept, and *Porgy and Bess* he never started to shoot. I have nothing against him, however, he made some very good films and it's an unfortunate thing that happened to him.

ANATOMY OF A MURDER. 1959. *Director:* Otto Preminger. *Screenplay:* Wendell Mayes. *Based on the novel by:* Robert Traver. *Photo-*

ANATOMY OF A MURDER:
James Stewart, Eve Arden, and Arthur O'Connell

graphy: Sam Leavitt. *Production Designer:* Boris Leven. *Editor:* Louis R. Loeffler. *Music:* Duke Ellington. *Wardrobe Designers:* Michael Harte, Vou Lee Giokaris. *Costume Supervision:* Hope Bryce. *Titles:* Saul Bass. *Producer:* Otto Preminger. *Production:* Carlyle Production. *Release:* Columbia, July 1, 1959. 160 mins. *Players:* James Stewart (*Paul Biegler*), Lee Remick (*Laura Manion*), Ben Gazzara (*Lt. Frederick Manion*), Joseph N. Welch (*Judge Weaver*), Kathryn Grant (*Mary Pilant*), Arthur O'Connell (*Parnell McArthy*), Eve Arden (*Maida Rutledge*), George C. Scott (*Claude Dancer*), Brooks West (*Mitch Lodwick*), Orson Bean (*Dr.*

ANATOMY OF A MURDER:
Stewart, Arden, Lee Remick and Ben
Gazzara

Smith), John Qualen (*Sulo, The
Guard*), Murray Hamilton (*Alphonse
Paquette*), Russ Brown (*Mr. Lemon*),
Don Ross (*Duane Miller*), Jimmy
Conlin (*Clarence Madigan*), Ned
Weaver (*Dr. Roschid*), Ken Lynch
(*Sgt. Duro*), Joseph Kearns (*Mr.
Lloyd Burke*), Howard McNear (*Dr.
Dompierre*), Royal Beal (*Sheriff*),
Duke Ellington (*Pie-Eye*), James
Water (*Army Sergeant*), Lloyd Le
Vasseur (*Court Employee*), Alexander
Campbell (*Dr. Harcourt*), Irving
Kupcinet (*Distinguished Gentleman*),
Mrs. Welch (*A Juror*).

Story

Frederick Manion, a Lieutenant in
the army, is arrested for the murder of a
bartender, Barney Quill. He claims, in
his defence, that the victim had raped
his wife Laura and beaten her up. Although Laura supports her husband's
story, the Police surgeon can find no
evidence that she has been raped.
Manion is defended by Paul Biegler,
a rather shabby small-town lawyer.
During the course of interviews, Biegler
discovers that Manion is violently possessive and jealous, and also that his
wife has a reputation for giving her
favours to other men. Biegler realises
that the Prosecution will try to make
the court believe that Laura was the
lover of the bartender and that Manion
killed him and beat her up when he discovered them together. Manion pleads
"not guilty" and Biegler, who knows
that his case is weak, sets his assistants
to try to find a witness who will save
Manion. Eventually he does so, and the
jury finds the Lieutenant not guilty by
reason of temporary insanity. After the
trial, Manion disappears without paying his fee to Biegler.

Preminger: In the book the woman
was older than the man. And I cast
Lana Turner—she was signed. We
had a conflict because I selected a
pair of slacks, and she didn't want to
wear them. She wanted to have her
costumes done by Jean Louis. I felt
that the wife of a second lieutenant
couldn't afford Jean Louis. Her agent
came to talk to me, and I said, "Look,
if she doesn't like it she can turn the

picture down." He thought I was bluffing. But I never am. He called me back and said she wouldn't wear the trousers. So I signed Lee Remick.

Six Years Later: Preminger's TV Battle

At the moment I'm involved in a lawsuit, for principle, not for money, concerning the right of a director to final cutting and editing of his film. This right now goes beyond the completion of a film for theatres; it should be extended to the showing of films on television.

Columbia Pictures sold or licensed one of my pictures, *Anatomy of a Murder*, to television and permitted these television stations to cut my picture at their discretion, when I claim my contract forbids the cutting of my films without my knowledge, permission or approval.

I am not at all against showing films on television, but I am against two practices: one, the elimination and cutting of pictures according to what they call "time slots." If they don't have the time, they shouldn't show the film.

To take a film that's two hours long and to cut half an hour from it to accommodate the commercials, this I am against. Secondly, I'm against the censorship these stations exercise, when they argue that objectionable scenes must not be seen in the living room. Certain films should be shown at night time perhaps, when children are in bed, but ultimately it is for parents to care for their children. This cutting is all nonsense, just a convenience for these TV people who actually don't care what they show as long as they have the chance to keep people at a set and show them commercials.

I'm not against commercials, either, but I do wish TV officials here would adopt the system they have in countries like England and France, where commercials are shown only at the beginning and the end, and on some occasions in the middle. However, if the necessity for these commercials interruptions really exists,

James Stewart in ANATOMY OF A MURDER

at least I, as the film-maker, and every other film-maker, should have the right to determine where the film should be interrupted and least harmed by these interruptions. How appalling that in the telling of the story, even when the tale is not five minutes old, it is stopped for two or four "messages" for detergents, hair lotions, medicines, cigarettes and deodorants. If films are made specially for television the story can be devised to accommodate them, like plays divided into acts with intermission. But feature films were never made to be interrupted like this.

In New York, Los Angeles and Chicago where *Anatomy of a Murder* was shown, it was interrupted as many as thirteen times for twenty-nine commercials. It is quite obvious that this kind of interruption is a mutilation of the film, that and nothing more. The judge gave me a temporary injunction and ruled that the film must be shown uncut, but he did not forbid the commercials. The case will come to court in about three weeks [*Preminger lost*].

It is quite true that I get a great deal of money from these showings, but still I prefer not to have the money nor to have the film shown under these circumstances. While I don't think that all films will live forever, once they are shown on TV they lose their life because they are rarely shown whole and seldom go back to theatres.

I do believe the public is also very aggravated by these commercials. You read letters to the editor every day on the subject. While they are not going to launch a nation-wide campaign or go on strike, eventually I really believe that this very bad practice of the interruption with loud, frequently offensive commercials will have to stop.

At the moment, hundreds of technicians across the country who care little about films make the cuts and the interruptions and so you have hundreds of different versions of the same film. This too is very wrong, to say nothing of the damage being done to a film-maker's reputation. Audiences are seeing a film in a way I did not intend them to see it. It is not my film any more; it is misrepresentation of my film, a fraud committed against the public.

This is only the beginning. Already George Stevens, Alfred Hitchcock and Howard Hawks have started suits to have their films shown uncut. I was grateful to Johnny Carson when on his television show he protested the mutilation of *Anatomy of a Murder*. If some film-makers fear loss of revenue they should remember that television cannot do without movies and if we all are united and said "no films unless shown whole with a minimum of interruptions" then television officials would have to agree. We should then receive our revenues and have our films shown properly.

It is shortsighted to grab the money now out of greed and without regard for the consequences. It will be a long fight, it will take time, but in the end, if television stations want my films they will have them only when they play them my way.

CBC New York, 711 Fifth Avenue, December 1965.

EXODUS. 1960. *Director :* Otto Preminger. *Screenplay :* Dalton Trumbo. *Based on the novel* "Exodus" *by :* Leon Uris. *Photography* (Super-Panavision 70, Technicolor): Sam Leavitt. *Art Directors :* Richard Day, Bill Hutchinson. *Set Director :* Dario Simoni. *Special Effects :* Cliff Richardson. *Editor :* Louis R. Loeffler. *Sound :* Paddy Cunningham, John Cox, Red Law. *Sound Effects :* Win Ryder. *Assistant Director :* Gerry O'Hara. *Music :* Ernest Gold. *Wardrobe Designers :* Joe King, May Walding, Margo Slater, Rudi Gernreich (for Eva Marie Saint). *Costume Supervisor :* Hope Bryce. *Make-up :* George Lane. *Hairstyles :* A. G. Scott. *Titles :* Saul Bass. *Producer :* Otto Preminger. *Assistant to the Producer :* Max Slater. *General Manager :* Martin Shute. *Production Manager :* Eva Monley. *Production :* Carlyle/Alpha Produc-

tion. *Release :* United Artists, March 27, 1960. 212 mins. (Filmed in Israel.) *Players :* Paul Newman (*Ari Ben Canaan*), Eva Marie Saint (*Kitty Fremont*), Ralph Richardson (*General Sutherland*), Peter Lawford (*Major Caldwell*), Lee J. Cobb (*Barak Ben Canaan*), Sal Mineo (*Dov Landau*), John Derek (*Taha*), Hugh Griffith (*Mandria*), David Opatoshu (*Akiva*), Jill Haworth (*Karen*), Gregory Ratoff (*Lakavitch*), Felix Aylmer (*Dr. Lieberman*), Marius Goring (*Von Storch*), Alexandra Stewart (*Jordana*), Michael Wager (*David*), Martin Benson (*Mordekai*), Paul Stevens (*Reuben*), Betty Walker (*Sarah*), Martin

Eva Marie Saint, Peter Lawford, and Ralph Richardson in EXODUS

Miller (*Dr. Odenheim*), Victor Maddern (*Sergeant*), George Maharis (*Yaov*), John Crawford (*Hank*), Samuel Segal (*Proprietor*), Dahn Ben Motz (*Uzi*), Peter Madden (*Dr. Clement*), Ralph Truman (*Colonel*), Joseph Furst (*Avidan*), Paul Stassino (*Driver*), Marc Burns (*Lt. O'Hara*), Esther Reichstadt (*Mrs. Hirshberg*), Zeporah Peled (*Mrs. Frankel*), Philo Hauser (*Novak*).

Story

In 1947 some thirty thousand Jews who have fled from Europe are interned by the British on the island of Cyprus and denied entry into Palestine. However, under the leadership of Ari Ben Canaan, a young officer of the Hagannah (Palestine's Jewish Underground), a plan is afoot to demonstrate to the world that Jews are willing to die for their freedom. After careful preparations, six hundred of them escape from an internment camp, board an old freighter called the "Exodus," go on a hundred-hour hunger strike in protest at the British destroyers blocking their path, and threaten to blow themselves out of the water if British troops board the ship.

Also aboard the "Exodus" is an American nurse, Kitty Fremont, who, while investigating the death of her newspaperman-husband, has become attached to a refugee child named Karen. Eventually, influenced by the sympathetic intervention of the island commander, General Sutherland, the British permit the "Exodus" to sail for Haifa.

Once in Palestine, a strong bond of affection develops between Ari and Kitty and the young woman learns of the internal conflict among the Jews themselves. Ari and his father, Barak, are staunch defenders of the Hagannah, which tries, when possible, to avoid the use of violence. Others, including Ari's uncle Akiva and a young former Auschwitz prisoner named Dov Landau, are members of the Irgun, a terrorist organisation.

Ari, despite his beliefs, joins with the Irgun in designing and executing a mass breakout of Jews from the Acre prison. Though the escape is successful, Akiva is fatally wounded.

Shortly afterwards, on November 29, 1947, the United Nations votes for the partition of Palestine. Almost immediately the Arabs, provoked by some former Nazis, institute a series of raids and attacks. As hostilities increase, Kitty decides not to return to America but to remain by Ari's side.

During a Syrian raid both Karen and Taha, a life-long Arab friend of Ari's, are killed. Their bodies are laid side by side in a common grave over which Ari delivers an impassioned eulogy. Then, accompanied by Kitty, he picks up his rifle and goes off to continue the fight for freedom.

Preminger: I tried, through very thorough research, to find out the exact truth, or the exact facts of events which form the background of *Exodus*, the historic events which led to the birth of the nation of Israel. But the story and the characters are in this picture also fictitious. They are based on a novel, which was the biggest best seller in the United States since *Gone with the Wind*, and I, as usual and as you very aptly observed, tried to make the characters beyond the novel, very real. I tried to get the motivations right. I tried to have people behave the way normal people would behave in life. Then I had to consider national feelings, but I made no compromise. The book was in many, many incidents anti-British and exaggerated, also anti-Arab. I made my research and I found out in many talks with Israelis who lived through this time (it is after all very recent history) that their feelings toward the British now are very friendly. As a matter of fact, there is almost a unanimous consent that any other nation would have been much rougher on Israel, and much more difficult in that conflict that existed, and exists in the picture, between a nation holding the mandate from the United Nations over Palestine, and a young nation that was fighting for homeland. I achieved this through a few changes from the book, without any really

Paul Newman in EXODUS

very deep or strong compromises, and I think that my picture (in these matters at least) is much closer to the truth, and to the historic facts, than is the book. It also avoids propaganda. It's an American picture, after all, that tries to tell the story, giving both sides a chance to plead their side. This leads to a danger which you are very well aware of, that is, in doing something like this and in presenting both sides of the question, events are apt to look contrived . . . a good person here, who is balanced by a bad one over there, and the other way round.

There again with the truth, it cannot look pat; these are, after all, events that have happened very recently and anybody (who wants to) can check them. For instance, I have two very important British characters. One is a general played by Sir Ralph Richardson, who is sympathetic to the cause of these Israelis, of the Jews, but still never gives up explaining the case of the British, and the predicament they actually were in by having accepted, years before, this mandate, and by having, also, to treat the Arabs justly. And then I have one other British officer, Peter Lawford, who is frankly anti-Semitic, and we tried to make this humorous and entertaining and I don't think that anybody would take offence to that. I got very, very reassuring comment from very many people in Israel, and here in America. Wherever the picture has opened, it was a very big success. It was not only the initial interest, but we have been playing now for ten weeks, and wherever we play we have never closed an engagement. And wherever we played, let's say three quarters of the engagement is sold out, and the last quarter of the engagement is very close to selling out, so there is an interest. I'm not saying this because of the grosses. I'm saying this because it is very satisfying for a man who makes a picture to see that people are interested in what he has made and come to see it. That's what we are doing it for, after all.

This film is in colour and for a very, very wide screen. I used the new Panavision 65 millimetre film and lenses, and it was very, very nice. I don't think that we lost any intimacy in the small scenes, and I feel that we achieved great scope in the scenes where we wanted to show the background—Palestine, Cyprus, the harbour, Famagusta, and I am extremely happy with this system, and when I have a story that again lends itself, I will definitely use it. I prefer it to any others. If you remember, I made *Porgy and Bess* in Todd-AO, but I found this system much easier to handle and much more satisfactory, as far as the technical side is concerned. Going from the standard wide screen to this large screen, it is easy to get bogged down and very static. I just forget that it's a large screen and handle it the way I want to see it on the screen. The additional fact was that we made this picture, of course, all in real locales. There is not one set in it. Everything was shot where it took place. We had a re-construction of a historic prison break. We shot it in the fortress of Acre where the prison break took place originally and we dynamited exactly the same wall, which was dynamited when the inmates broke out in 1947 and then we rebuilt it again, as it was after that prison break. This gives also a certain authenticity and a feeling of reality to the story, which I feel was very necessary to show that we really tried to tell the truth, and we just didn't make up a story.

Whether I approve of violence or not (and I don't approve of it), the state of Israel would not have come into being without the terrorists. Every revolution needs some kind of terror or violence in order to unseat the *régime*. That's why I also understand what's going on in the Negro movement now, but I don't approve of it. It might momentarily hurt the Negro cause, but a revolution is not something logical that you can figure out.

I had a big argument in Israel when I made the picture. The ruling group did not like the idea that I gave any credit in the picture to the terrorists. Later, the terrorists also made it difficult for me. They felt they did not get enough credit, and even threatened to picket that big scene I did on the square with forty thousand people. I didn't let myself be swayed by either side, and I felt that it was the right balance.

When I did *Exodus* (this also happened on *The Man with the Golden Arm*), the original author denounced me. When we started, I had engaged Mr. Uris to write the screenplay. I very quickly realised he couldn't write it, at least not the way *I* wanted it. I don't think he can write dialogue.

I think he has a very good imagination —he's what I'd call a "passionate story-teller." But in telling a story he becomes too much of a partisan.

You see, I would be willing to defend my film of *Exodus* against some really big enemies of Israel, like Nasser. I would be willing to sit down with him, and let him tell me why he felt this picture was unfair. Because I know it isn't. But the book by Uris has a pox against all the enemies of the Jews in it, and that is difficult to defend. This is part of my whole outlook on the world: I am basically an optimist. I don't believe that there are any real villains. If somebody is a villain, I try to find out why. I don't necessarily excuse him, but I try to understand him.

People often come to me and ask if the film is going to be faithful to the book. "Faithful to the book." Once an author sells (and "sells" is a very hard word) the film rights, he gives up any claim to have somebody do it "faithfully." By that time, my mind and my talent and my heart are in charge of this story and these people. They become my raw material, and I can only re-create them the way I see them. It would be different if the author came to me and said, "Look, you want to do this book; let's be partners. Let's do it together, and we will have equal say."

CBC, New York February 24, 1961

ADVISE AND CONSENT. 1962. *Director:* Otto Preminger. *Screenplay:* Wendell Mayes. *Based on the novel* "Advise and Consent" *by:* Allen Drury. *Photography* (Panavision): Sam Leavitt. *Art Director:* Lyle R. Wheeler. *Set Director:* Eli Benneche. *Editor:* Louis R. Loeffler. *Sound:* Harold Lewis, William Hamilton. *Sound Effects:* Leon Birnbaum. *Assistant Director:* L. V. McCardle Jr. *Music:* Jerry Fielding. *Title Song, lyrics by:* Ned Washington. *Sung by:* Frank Sinatra. *Technical Advisor:* Allen Drury. *Titles:* Saul Bass. *Wardrobe Designers:* Joe King, Adele Parmenter, Michael Harte, Bill Blass (for Gene Tierney).

ADVISE AND CONSENT: Charles Laughton harangues; Walter Pidgeon and Paul Ford listen

Costume Co-Ordinator: Hope Bryce. *Hairstyles:* Myrl Stoltz. *Make-up:* Del Armstrong, Robert Jiras. *Producer:* Otto Preminger. *Assistant to the Producer:* Max Slater. *Production Manager:* Jack McEdward. *Production:* An Alpha-Alpina Production. *Release:* Columbia Pictures, June, 1962. 140 mins. (Location scenes filmed in Washington, D.C.) *Players:* Henry Fonda (*Robert Leffingwell*), Charles Laughton (*Senator Seabright Cooley*), Don Murray (*Senator Brigham Anderson*), Walter Pidgeon (*Senator Bob Munson*), Peter Lawford (*Senator Lafe Smith*), Gene Tierney (*Dolly Harrison*), Franchot Tone (*The President*), Lew Ayres (*The Vice-President*), Burgess Meredith (*Herbert Gelman*), Eddie Hodges (*Johnny Leffingwell*), Paul Ford (*Senator Stanley Danta*), George Grizzard (*Senator Fred Van Ackerman*), Inga Swenson (*Ellen Anderson*), Paul McGrath (*Hardiman Fletcher*), Will Geer (*Senate Minority Leader*), Edward Andrews (*Senator Orrin Knox*), Betty White (*Senator Bessie Adams*), Malcolm Atterbury (*Senator Tom August*), J. Edward McKinley (*Senator Powell Hanson*), William Quinn (*Senator Paul Hendershot*), Tiki Santos (*Senator Kanaho*), Raoul de Leon (*Senator Velez*), Tom Helmore (*British Ambassador*), Hilary Eaves (*Lady Maudulayne*), René Paul (*French Ambassador*), Michelle Montau (*Cele-*

stine Barre), Raj Mallick (*Indian Ambassador*), Russ Brown (*Night Watchman*), Paul Stevens (*Louis Newborn*), Janet Jane Carty (*Pidge Anderson*), Chet Stratton (*Rev. Carney Birch*), Larry Tucker (*Manuel*), John Granger (*Ray Shaff*), Sid Gould (*Bartender*), Bettie Johnson (*Lafe's Girl*), Cay Forester (*President's Secretary*), William H. Y. Knighton Jr. (*President of White House Correspondent's Association*), Hon. Henry Fountain Ashurst (*Senator McCafferty*), Hon. Guy M. Gillette (*Senator Harper*).

Story

An obstinate, self-willed President of the United States, knowing that he has not long to live, asks the U.S. Senate to "advise and consent" to the appointment, as Secretary of State, of the highly controversial Robert Leffingwell. Southern Senator Seabright Coo-

Preminger emphasises a point to Charles Laughton on the set of ADVISE AND CONSENT

ley holds a long standing personal grudge against Leffingwell, and does what he can to prevent the appointment. He produces a mentally unbalanced clerk, Herbert Gelman, who swears that he knew Leffingwell years ago as a co-member of a Communist cell.

Although Leffingwell confesses the truth of this accusation to the President, it is dismissed as a youthful indiscretion, and Leffingwell denies the accusation while testifying under oath before a Senate sub-committee. The committee chairman, Brigham Anderson, learns of the perjury and demands that Leffingwell's nomination be withdrawn. When the President refuses, Anderson decides that for the good of the country he must make the truth public.

Before he can do so, however, he is threatened with blackmail by Fred Van Ackerman, an overly-ambitious young senator who warns Anderson that if he fails to approve the nomination his own youthful indiscretion—a wartime homosexual experience in Hawaii—will be exposed.

Unable to face the shame of his own past and unable to confess the truth to his wife, Anderson commits suicide. Following the tragic news the Senate votes on Leffingwell's nomination. It ends in a deadlock, with the decisive vote going to the Vice-President. As he ponders his decision, word arrives that the President has died. The once ineffectual man is suddenly inspired by the monumental responsibility of his new-found office and he declines to vote. "I'd prefer," he says, "to name my own Secretary of State."

Preminger, on the set of Advise and Consent, replies to questions about Edward R. Murrow's statement in Washington that Hollywood should create a favourable "film image" of Americans for showing abroad:

I am frankly quite surprised, knowing Mr. Murrow and his past and his fight for freedom of expression that he should now, having a job in the government, try to restrict the freedom of expression of the screen, even in a very mild or friendly way. I think it is underrating foreign countries and their people if we believe that by painting a picture of America rose-coloured, we would in any way be successful. I feel that our weapon is truth. I feel that showing America as it is, with all its good sides, its democracy and freedom and on the other hand, not hiding our problems, not hiding our criticism of our own institutions, will make it clear to foreign countries, to people all over the world, that we have freedom of expression. New countries which have a choice between Russian propaganda and American truth will, I'm quite sure, decide for our way of life. I was in Russia recently, and there were many conversations about the difference

Preminger on location in Washington, with Laughton, Pidgeon and Don Murray in background

between our attitude on motion pictures and theirs. They pointed out to me that they considered motion pictures as a means of education, which is in a way also a word for propaganda. While we don't do this, it doesn't mean that we don't put any meaning into our pictures. It means that we may in a subtle way also be trying to project our thoughts, but without forcing them on audiences, leaving it to the public to draw their own conclusions. With *Advise and Consent* I think that many people can draw many different conclusions. I hope, if I have succeeded with my picture that it is not just one-sided.

QUESTION: In a recent investigation of Hollywood's runaway problems, a House sub-committee said that they were going to come back early next year and consider the possibility of a government subsidy for movies. Do you think that's a good or a bad idea?

PREMINGER: I think it's a very

bad idea. I am convinced from a practical point of view that we will never get the subsidy because this is basically so much against American tradition, this is part of our free competitive system.

QUESTION: The Catholic Bishops' Committee recently suggested that we have classification. Are you in favour of classification?

PREMINGER: Yes, there is the paradox of my position. While I am violently against censorship, I am very much for voluntary, individual classification. This is the responsibility of producers (and I have been doing this for years). I would give *Advise and Consent* adult classification, and when I say "adult," I mean that younger people, let's say people under sixteen, should not be permitted to go to see this picture, except in company of their parents. There are not any scenes of excessive violence or love-making, but there is a homosexual theme throughout the picture. There are young people who don't know about homosexuality and might not understand. They might have to ask older people what this is all about, but some parents might not want their children to see anything, or to know anything about homosexuality. I know that parents like this exist, but it is their right to bring up their children their way. *Interview released by Columbia, 1962.*

THE CARDINAL. 1963. *Director:* Otto Preminger. *Screenplay:* Robert Dozier. *Based on the novel by:* Henry Morton Robinson. *Photography* (Panavision, Technicolor): Leon Shamroy. *Second Unit Photography:* Piero Portalupi. *Production Designer:* Lyle Wheeler. *Art Directors:* Otto Niedermoser (Vienna sequences), Antonio Sarzi-Braga (Rome sequences). *Set Directors:* Gene Callahan, Guilio Sperabene. *Editor:* Louis R. Loeffler. *Sound:* Harold Lewis, Red Law, Walter Goss, Morris Feingold. *Assistant Directors:* Gerry O'Hara, Bob Vietro, Bryan Coates, Hermann Leitner, Robert Fiz, Eric von Stroheim Jr. *Music:* Jerome Moross. *Music Co-ordinator:* Leon Birnbaum. *The Song* "They Haven't Got the Girls in the U.S.A." *lyrics by:* Al Stillman; *music by:* Jerome Moross; *sung by:* Bobby Morse. *Liturgical Chants for ordination, consecration and religious service by:* the Friars of Casamari Monastery, under the direction of Dom Nivardo Bultarazzi (Priest) and Dom Raffaele Scaccia (Prior). "Alleluia" *from the motet* "Exultate Jubilate" *by* Mozart, *sung by:* the Wiener Jugendchor; *soloist:* Wilma Lipp. *Script supervisor:* Kathleen Fagan. *Wardrobe Designer:*

Opposite: Preminger directing THE CARDINAL

Tom Tryon with John Huston in THE CARDINAL

Donald Brooks. *Costume Co-ordinator:* Hope Bryce. *Choreography:* Buddy Schwats. *Titles:* Saul Bass. *Technical Advisor:* Donald Hayne. *Producer:* Otto Preminger. *Executive Assistant to the Producer:* Nat Rudich. *Associate Producer:* Martin G. Schute. *Production Managers:* Harrison Starr, Eva Monley, Henry Weinberger, Paul Waldher (Danubia Films, Vienna), Guy Luongo (International Film Services, Rome). *Production:* Gamma. An Otto Preminger Production. *Release:* Columbia, December, 1963. 175 mins. (Filmed in Boston, Stamford, Rome, Vienna and Hollywood.) *Players:* Tom Tryon (*Stephen Fermoyle*).

BOSTON:
Carol Lynley (*Mona Fermoyle*), Dorothy Gish (*Celia*), Maggie McNamara (*Florrie*), Bill Hayes (*Frank*), Cameron Prud'Homme (*Din*), Cecil Kellaway (*Monsignor Monaghan*), Loring Smith (*Cornelius J. Deegan*), John Saxon (*Benny Rampell*), John Huston (*Cardinal Glennon*), Jose Duval (*Ramon Gongaro*), Peter MacLean (*Father Callahan*), Robert Morse (*Bobby and His Adora-Belles*), James Hickman (*Father Lyons*), Berenice Gahm (*Mrs. Rampell*), Billy Reed (*Master of Ceremonies*).
L'ENCLUME:
Pat Henning (*Hercule Menton*), Burgess Meredith (*Father Ned Halley*), Jill Haworth (*Lalage Menton*), Russ Brown (*Dr. Heller*).
ROME:
Raf Vallone (*Cardinal Quarenghi*), Tullio Carminati (*Cardinal Giacobbi*) Ossie Davis (*Father Gillis*), Don Francesco Mancini of Veroli (*M.C. at Ordination*), Dino Di Luca (*Italian Monsignor*).
NEW YORK PIER:
Carol Lynley (*Regina Fermoyle*), Donald Hayne (*Father Eberling*).
LAMAR, GEORGIA:
Chill Wills (*Monsignor Whittle*), Arthur Hunnicutt (*Sheriff Dubrow*), Doro Merande (*Woman Picket*), Patrick O'Neal (*Cecil Turner*), Murray Hamilton (*Lafe*).
VIENNA:
Romy Schneider (*Annemarie*), Peter

Weck (*Kurt von Hartman*), Rudolph Forster (*Drunk Man at the Ball*), Josef Meinrad (*Cardinal Innitzer*), Dagmar Schmedes (*Madame Walter*), Eric Frey (*Seyss-Inquart*), Josef Krastel (*Von Hartman's Butler*), Mathias Fuchs (*Father Neidermoser*), Vilma Degischer (*Sister Wilhelmina*), Wolfgang Preiss (*S.S. Major*), Jurgen Wilke (*Army Lieutenant*), Wilma Lipp (*Soloist*).

Story

In 1917 Stephen Fermoyle is ordained as a Roman Catholic priest and returns to his native Boston as a curate. When his sister Mona decides to marry a Jewish boy, Benny, the Irish Catholic Fermoyles are aghast. Mona runs away and becomes the partner of a night club tango dancer.

Meanwhile, because of his intellectual arrogance, Stephen falls foul of the Archbishop of Glennon, head of the Boston diocese, and is relegated to a poor country parish, L'Enclume, where he learns a lesson in humility from Father Ned Halley. News comes that Mona is about to give birth to an illegitimate child, and the doctor announces that she can be saved only if the child's cranium is crushed. Following Catholic dogma, Stephen refuses permission, and Mona dies.

Disturbed by this incident, and newly appointed by Glennon to the Vatican diplomatic corps, Stephen decides to leave the Church, but is persuaded by Glennon to take a year's leave of absence. Teaching languages in Vienna he has a romantic interlude with a student, Annemarie, but decides that the church is his true vocation.

He returns to Rome where he befriends a Negro priest, Father Gillis, returns with him to Georgia, and helps to strike a blow for Negro emancipation against the Ku-Klux-Klan.

Subsequently, promoted to the rank of Bishop, he is sent on a diplomatic mission to Vienna to persuade Cardinal Innitzer, head of the Austrian diocese, to oppose the Nazi infiltration. Here he meets Annemarie again—now married—and witnesses her arrest by the Gestapo. The Nazis have already gained a strong foothold in Austria, and Stephen has to leave, his mission unsuccessful.

On the eve of the Second World War, he is appointed Cardinal, and assumes the robes of office, determined "to do his utmost to help America unite with the church in the never-ceasing fight for political and religious freedom."

Preminger: The question of who is the author of the picture, the producer, the director or the writer, depends actually on the set up and on the personalities. As you know, I am an independent producer. I have been since I made *The Moon Is Blue* in 1953, and I choose my stories, I choose my themes, and I choose them only according to my own instinct. I don't think we can calculate what will be successful, I only hope that what interests me, I can re-create on the screen in a way that will interest other people and therefore be successful. I used the word "re-create" advisedly, because I feel that I am not an illustrator of books, or just an interpreter of a play, even if my picture is based on a play. I feel that I have the right to re-create it, with the help of a writer. Now if you ask how much the writer contributes, he contributes very much, but I work very closely with the writer. The procedure in motion pictures is different from novels or plays, where the writer starts out to write original works. The writer is engaged for a film and naturally there has to be a meeting of the minds between the director, or the producer/director (I don't really believe in titles) and the writer. In *The Cardinal*, we worked eighteen months on the script until it was to my satisfaction and then I shot the script exactly as it is. Now I don't want to take anything away from the writer, but if you really ask whose thoughts are mainly represented, or whose personality is represented in the picture, I must claim this, for better or for worse. I will not only claim the praise, but also take the blame.

There are many significant statements in this film about the church, about politics, about racial segregation. These things concern me deeply. People have often asked me why my pictures are what you call "controversial." Well, they are not really controversial any more than anything that is present-day is controversial. Now I am trying, when I take a story like *The Cardinal*, to show both sides, because I am convinced that in any dramatic medium we must show both sides, otherwise there is no conflict and no drama. But on the other hand, naturally it will always come out the way I feel it should. In other words, when I show the racial persecution in the South in some of the scenes in the picture (which is by the way based on the book) it is quite clear that I feel any racial segregation or persecution is unfair and also old-fashioned. I simply feel that any intelligent man who can look into the future knows that whatever difficulties it might cause, we are in a revolution, really, where all this racial nonsense must disappear. That is my personal opinion, and I think that pictures eventually must show it. I show the other side, too, from the point of view of the Church. Now the Church was always an institution that interested me deeply. The last play that I directed before I left Vienna in 1935 was about the Jesuit Order. It was called *The First Legion* with Albert Bassermann, and I feel it's a very fascinating institution. Now I know more about it, working very closely in Rome and in Vienna and also partly in Boston, in America, with the Catholic Church and the people of the Catholic Church, and I am fascinated by the autonomy and the freedom within this very strict hierarchy. In many ways the Church is liberal, and I tried to show this too. People are permitted, within the Church, according to their position, of course, to have their personal opinions. I show my hero moving from a rather immature man who takes everything literally to a mature man who knows how to combine his own feelings with the laws of the Church, and to live within the Church without giving up his own personality or hurting his own conscience.

Tryon with Romy Schneider in THE CARDINAL

We shot only two scenes in the studios. One was in the projection room which for technical reasons had to be in the studio, because we have to interlock the projection machine and the camera, and then the sequence where, in Vienna, the mob destroys the Cardinal's Palace. While we had permission to shoot in the Cardinal's Palace in Vienna and we did shoot in it, downstairs, when it came to destroying the upstairs, I built an exact replica, because I couldn't pos-

sibly destroy the Cardinal's Palace; but even the picture that you see slashed is a copy of a picture that was slashed then, and hangs now with the torn pieces hanging down in the Palace. They kept it there, in memory of those riots, in 1938. The projection room was done in the studio in Rome and the other scenes in Vienna, in the studio, because all the people were in Vienna and I had to have the same extras to connect it. Now, the logistics of a picture like this are very tough, because we shot in Boston, in Vienna and in Rome. We had a very big American crew, about thirty-five people, travelling with us, and we were supplemented everywhere by local technicians. We were very lucky, we didn't shoot the picture too long, and it worked.

We went to the Vatican, and this film was shot in a former residence of the Pope, the summer residence, which has the same architecture, as the old offices in the Vatican used to have (the offices were rebuilt in 1952 and are now very modern small rooms) but we needed naturally the offices of that time. As they were not available any more, the Vatican gave us this summer residence, which is now a museum, and we furnished it as the offices were furnished (there are photographs and all that) and it made it look real. It is pretty authentic. All the sequences in churches, like the consecration of the hero as a bishop, or the vows, when he becomes a priest, all this was done, not by extras, but by real seminarists and priests in Rome under the supervision of the real Masters of Ceremonies for these ceremonies, so they too are really authentic.

Everywhere in the world I found old cars. People collect them. As a matter of fact, Cardinal Innitzer's car is an old car which is kept there, and which he and a chancellor of the Austrian Republic actually used, you know, Chancellor Schusnic, and this automobile manufacturer is keeping this like a museum piece and permits only the one driver, who was then with the car, and is now employed by him to drive it; so he played the driver in the picture. In Boston we got some of the streetcars from a museum and we shot inside the streetcar, no back projection. There's not one shot with back projection in the picture.

The home of Tryon's father was inside a real home too. We found the little house in that district, in that part of Boston, and we furnished it. It was not furnished like this, naturally, in the style of the times, of the period. They are all real rooms and real interiors and exteriors. When the priest went to take up his new post in Massachusetts, where Burgess Meredith was living, people were living in the railway carriages. A wretched existence. I put some more railway carriages there because I needed it close, and I was lucky because I needed snow for this scene, and the night before I started to shoot, before it was scheduled, it started to snow. Pictorially, these scenes I think were very beautiful. To make it look real, we must select. My art director, Lyle Wheeler, and I, we travelled, first alone, and selected the sites. He travelled first, and he gave me a choice. Then I approved the sites. Then we brought the cameraman, so he knew in advance where he will be able to put the lights. You know, the preparation of a picture is really more work than the shooting of a picture. We recorded all the sound while we were filming too. Some of the sound is hollow, but I prefer it because it's natural. When you talk in rooms like that, it is not as perfect as in a studio. I think it is better if these things are not too perfect. I find that sound that is too perfect is also monotonous. And I am very careful not to destroy it at the end, when the sound is being re-recorded and everything is being combined. I try to keep the feeling, like when you interview me. You could take this interview and smooth it out, and the sound would sound probably, to an engineer, much better; but you would lose the vitality of our conversation, which exists in people speaking louder or lower, faster or slower. While the audience is not exactly aware of it, sub-consciously it adds up to an impression of real life, which in this kind of picture I want to give.

When casting a picture, I naturally try to move away from everything that is commonplace, usual or conventional. There are some very good character actors who could have played Archbishop Glennon quite well, but the ones I wanted were not available, and those who were available, I felt would give predictable performances. So I was looking for somebody outside, somebody mentioned Huston, I liked the idea, and I called him. I was in Rome when I sent him the script, he just had time in those few weeks that we needed, and he thought it would be fun. I stopped in London and we shook hands, and he was a delight in every way. He was more professional than any actor I know and more conscientious. We have been friends for twenty years. People want to know about directing a director. He didn't act like a director. He acted like a very professional actor, he never complained about anything, he never made any suggestions. He rehearsed, he knew his lines, he was on time and it was wonderful. I used the actual ordination ceremonies to present the story in a flashback. It is a ceremony which if you played it out all the way through would be monotonous, because it really takes three hours, to read all these Latin letters, and therefore I used this time as a dramatic device. I felt he would think at this point of his life, of what had happened to him until now. It seemed natural.

CBC, New York, December 1963

I read the book thirteen years before I filmed it. I was fascinated by it, because I'm fascinated by institutions, from the Senate of the United States to the Catholic Church. I think the Catholic Church is a political institution. The way it's organised and works is ingenious. The Church is not a completely totalitarian government as you might think. It's true that the Pope has the final say on everything, but the wisdom is that he never acts like Adolf Hitler. You see, he always gives the lower echelons a lot of autonomy. It's an interesting mixture of totalitarianism and, perhaps not democracy, but individual autonomy.

IN HARM'S WAY. 1964. *Director :* Otto Preminger. *Screenplay :* Wendell Mayes. *Based on the novel by :* James Bassett. *Photography* (Panavision): Loyal Griggs. *Second Unit Photography :* Philip Lathrop. *Production Designer :* Lyle Wheeler. *Art Director :* Al Roelofs. *Set Directors :* Morris Hoffman, Richard Mansfield. *Special Effects :* Lawrence W. Butler. *Editors :* George Tomasini, Hugh S. Fowler. *Sound :* Harold Lewis, Charles Grenzbach. *Assistant Directors :* Daniel McCauley, Howard Joslin, Michael Davies. *Music :* Jerry Goldsmith. *Special Photography :* Farciot Edouart. *Titles :* Saul Bass. *Script Supervision :* Kathleen Fagan. *Costume Co-ordination :* Hope Bryce. *Producer :* Otto Preminger. *Assistant to the Producer :* Nat Rudich. *Production Managers :* Eva Monley, Henry Weinberger, Stanley H. Goldsmith, James Henderling. *Production :* Sigma Productions. *Release :* Paramount Pictures, April, 1965. 165 mins. *Players :* John Wayne (*Capt. Rockwell Torrey*), Kirk Douglas (*Cdr. Paul Eddington*), Patricia Neal (*Lt. Maggie Haynes*), Tom Tryon (*Lt. [jg] William McConnel*), Paula Prentiss (*Bev McConnel*), Brandon De Wilde (*Ens. Jeremiah Torrey*), Jill Haworth (*Ens. Annalee Dorne*), Dana Andrews (*Adm. Broderick*), Stanley Holloway (*Clayton Canfil*), Burgess Meredith (*Cdr. Powell*), Franchot Tone (*CINCPAC I Admiral*), Patrick O'Neal (*Cdr. Neal Owynn*), Carroll O'Connor (*Lt. Cdr. Burke*), Slim Pickens (*CPO Culpepper*), James Mitchum (*Ens. Griggs*), George Kennedy (*Col. Gregory*), Bruce Cabot (*Quartermaster Quoddy*), Barbara

Kirk Douglas with Jill Haworth in IN HARM'S WAY

Bouchet (*Liz Eddington*), Tod Andrews (*Capt. Tuthill*), Larry Hagman (*Lt. Cline*), Stewart Moss (*Ens. Balch*), Richard Le Pore (*Lt. Tom Agar*), Chet Stratton (*Ship's Doctor*), Soo Young (*Tearful Woman*), Dort Clark (*Boston*), Phil Mattingly (*P-T Boat Skipper*), Henry Fonda (*CINC-PAC II Admiral*).

Story

> "*I wish to have no connection with any ship that does not sail fast, for I intend to go in harm's way.*"
>
> *John Paul Jones*

When the *Japanese attack Pearl Harbor, Captain Rockwell Torrey assumes command of a few U.S. vessels and leads a sea attack against the invaders. But the battle is a disaster and Torrey returns to his base in disgrace. At the same time, his embittered executive officer, Commander Paul Eddington, learns that his unfaithful wife has been killed during the attack.*

As Torrey is grudgingly performing desk work but happily courting Nurse Maggie Haynes, word reaches him that his son Jere, whom he has not seen for years, is an officer serving nearby who harbours nothing but contempt for his father. When they eventually meet, Torrey is further disappointed to learn that Jere is a callow youth seeking a cushy appointment on the staff of Admiral Broderick, a weak and indecisive procrastinator.

John Wayne with Patricia Neal in
IN HARM'S WAY

As retaliatory naval operations are being set in motion, Torrey's true worth is recognised by top echelon brass and he is promoted to Admiral and put in charge of capturing several key islands, a spearhead mission which Broderick has been unable to accomplish.

Torrey's ultimate victory not only discredits Broderick, but also wins him the respect of Jere who asks to be transferred back to his PT boat unit. But tragedy strikes the young officer when Eddington, driven nearly insane by the memory of his wife's infidelity, drunkenly rapes Jere's girl friend Annalee, at a beach party.

When the girl commits suicide,

Eddington, to redeem himself, goes on an unauthorised mission and radios the exact size and location of the Japanese fleet before being shot down. During the ensuing first great sea battle of the war, Jere is killed and Torrey is badly wounded. Maggie cares for him aboard a hospital ship and although he loses a leg, he is assured that he will soon be back in action and in command of a task force headed for Tokyo.

Preminger: The old classic picture technique always cuts to reaction shots, particularly in comedies. I feel that underrates the audience. It's like putting in mechanical laughter on television. There's an example in *In Harm's Way*; when John Wayne tells Paula Prentiss that her husband is missing, I could have cut to her reaction, since she's facing away from the camera. Instead, she turns into the camera after a few seconds. It is my conviction that every cut interrupts the flow of story-telling. When I want a close-up, I either have the people come closer to the camera or move the camera closer to them. But always with some motivation, not wildly. You can cut without being too obvious, but it still interrupts the illusion, unless you want to use a cut to shock the audience. But this is only a theory, and I am an enemy of theory. By the way, that was Paula Prentiss's last scene in the picture, and she so much wanted to be good that she kept unconsciously kicking herself in the ankle. When the scene was over, she suddenly couldn't walk, and she was taken to the hospital. She had broken her ankle, but she was concentrating so hard on the scene that she didn't realise it.

BUNNY LAKE IS MISSING. 1965. *Director:* Otto Preminger. *Screenplay:* John and Penelope Mortimer. *Based on the novel by:* Evelyn Piper. *Photography* (Panavision): Denys Coop. *Production Designer:* Don Ashton. *Set Directors:* Elven Webb, Scott Slimon. *Special Effects:* Charles Staffell. *Editor:* Peter Thornton. *Sound:* Jonathan Bates. *Sound Recording:* Claude Hitchcock, Red Law. *Assistant Directors:* Bryan Coates, Bernie Williams, Ivo Nightingale. *Music:* Paul Glass. *Titles:* Saul Bass. *Costume Co-ordinator:* Hope Bryce. *Producer:* Otto Preminger. *Associate Producer:* Martin C. Shute. *Assistant to the Producer:* Max Slater. *Production:* Wheel Productions. *Release:* Columbia Pictures, October 3, 1965. 107 mins. (Filmed in England.) *Players:* Keir Dullea (*Stephen*), Carol Lynley (*Ann*), Laurence Olivier (*Newhouse*), Martita Hunt (*Ada Ford*), Noël Coward (*Wilson*), Lucie Mannheim (*Cook*), Adrienne Corri (*Dorothy*), Anna Massey (*Elvira*), Finlay Currie (*Doll-maker*), Clive

Revill (*Andrews*), Jill Melford (*Teacher*), Kika Markham (*Nurse*), Delphi Lawrence (*First mother at school*), Suzanne Neve (*Second mother at school*), Richard Wattis (*Clerk in shipping office*), Victor Maddern (*Taxi driver*), Fred Emney (*Man in Soho*), David Oxley (*Doctor*), Megs Jenkins (*Hospital Sister*), John Forbes-Robertson (*Hospital Attendant*), Damaris Hayman (*Daphne*), Jane Evers (*Policewoman*), Patrick Jordan (*Policeman*), John Sharp (*Fingerprint man*), Geoffrey Frederick (*Police Photographer*), Percy Herbert (*Policeman at Station*), Michael Wynne (*Rogers*), Bill Maxam (*Barman*), Tim Brinton (*Newscaster*), Themselves (*The Zombies*).

Keir Dullea with Carol Lynley in
BUNNY LAKE IS MISSING

Story

Ann Lake and her small daughter Bunny (four years old, illegitimate) are newcomers to London, setting up house with Ann's journalist brother Stephen. In the rush of moving from a borrowed house in Hampstead to a rented flat, Ann dumps Bunny somewhat abruptly at her new nursery school. When she goes back at lunchtime, no-one at the school is prepared to, admit that the child was ever there. Inspector Newhouse treats it as a routine disappearance, until he finds that all Bunny's possessions are missing from the flat. Noticing that Stephen Lake seems more concerned about his sister's state of mind than about the missing child, and learning that Ann once had an imaginary childhood playmate whom she called Bunny, Newhouse begins to doubt whether Bunny Lake actually exists.

Increasingly desperate, and determined somehow to prove that Bunny is real, Ann finds a toy-shop repair ticket for a broken doll and rushes off to the shop for this flimsy bit of proof. Stephen follows her, destroys the doll, knocks Ann cold and packs her off, still unconscious, to the hospital. Then he goes back to the Hampstead house to set about murdering Bunny, who has spent the day locked in the boot of his car. Intensely possessive about his sister,

Carol Lynley in BUNNY LAKE IS MISSING

tied by bonds more infantile than incestuous, he thinks the child has come between them.

Ann escapes from the hospital and follows him, but can't get Bunny away. All she can do is stave off Stephen's murderous impulses by enmeshing him in a round of childhood games. They are still at this when Newhouse, who has begun to suspect the truth, arrives with a rescue party.

Preminger: *Bunny Lake* was also not a successful film, but when it was shown on television I got many calls, letters and telegrams from people who told me how much they liked it, and they were sorry they didn't see it in theatres. There is one good thing people forget about television, and that is it helps to keep pictures alive and people interested in films.

It is a small story about a kidnapping. The mother of the little girl who has been kidnapped is unmarried and is unable to prove the existence of the child. The child's father will not admit to it because he is already married to another woman and pretends he does not know the mother. There is a certain social theme here; if you do not conform to the rules of society, the law does not protect you. That is an important part of the film.

I made no attempt in *Bunny Lake Is Missing* to create a London mood; with evocative shots of the city. I think people notice *Bunny Lake* is placed in London, but the fact that the story plays there is not particularly essential. It only made it easier because these two Americans were isolated. There were no friends, there were no people they knew from the past, and that made the suspense angle better. That's why I moved the story to London. Making the script sound believable was very difficult. When I worked on the original story, I found that the villain, the old woman who stole the child—the former teacher of the school—was uninteresting. It's a completely arbitrary solution; it doesn't make much sense. Then we created a rich heiress who manufactured this whole thing because she had no children and wanted a child. This also turned out to be terribly phony. I finally came to the conclusion that it would have to be somebody very close from the beginning. That was the third and final attempt.

HURRY SUNDOWN. 1966. *Director:* Otto Preminger. *Screenplay:* Thomas C. Ryan, Horton Foote. *Based on the novel by:* K. and B. Gilden. *Photography* (Panavision, Technicolor): Milton Krasner, Loyal Griggs. *Production Designer:* Gene Callahan. *Set Director:* John Godfrey. *Special Effects:* Willis Cook. *Editors:* Louis Loeffler, James D. Wells. *Sound:* Harold Lewis, Franklin Milton, Bertil Hallberg, Glenn Anderson. *Assistant Directors:* Burt Harris, Howard Joslin, John Avildsen. *Music:* Hugo Montenegro. *Wardrobe Designers:* Estevez. *Makeup:* Del Armstrong, Web Overlander. *Hairstyles:* Frederic Jones. *Producer:* Otto Preminger. *Assistant to the Producer:* Nat Rudich. *Production Managers:* Stephen F. Kesten, Eva Monley. *Production:* Sigma Productions. *Release:* Paramount Pictures, February 6, 1967. 146 mins. (Location scenes filmed in Louisiana; interiors at M-G-M.) *Players:* Michael Caine (*Henry Warren*), Jane Fonda (*Julie Ann Warren*), John

Phillip Law (*Rad McDowell*), Diahann Carroll (*Vivian Thurlow*), Robert Hooks (*Reeve Scott*), Faye Dunaway (*Lou McDowell*), Burgess Meredith (*Judge Purcell*), Jim Backus (*Carter Sillens*), Robert Reed (*Lars Finchley*), Beah Richards (*Rose Scott*), Rex Ingram (*Professor Thurlow*), Madeleine Sherwood (*Eula Purcell*), Doro Merande (*Ada Hemmings*), George Kennedy (*Sheriff Coombs*), Frank Converse (*Rev. Clem De Lavery*), Loring Smith (*Thomas Elwell*), Donna Danton (*Sukie Purcell*), John Mark (*Colie Warren*), Luke Askew (*Dolph Higginson*), Peter Goff (*Lipscomb*), William Elder (*Bishop*), Steve Sanders (*Charles McDowell*), Dawn Barcelona (*Ruby McDowell*), David Sanders (*Wyatt McDowell*), Michael Henry Roth (*Timmy McDowell*), Gladys Newman (*Mrs. Coombs*), Joan Parks (*Kissie*), Robert C. Bloodwell (*Ozzie Higginson*), Charles Keel (*Kenny*), Kelly Ross (*Dottie*), Ada Hall Covington (*Clara*), Gene Rutherford, Bill Hart, Dean Smith (*Hunt Club Members*).

Story

Following the Second World War, a northern cannery combine negotiates for the purchase of a large tract of uncultivated Georgia farmland. The major portion of the land is owned by Julie Ann Warren and has already been optioned by her unscrupulous, draftdodging husband, Henry. Now the

combine must also obtain two smaller plots—one owned by Henry's cousin Rad McDowell, a combat veteran with a wife and family; the other by Reeve Scott, a young Negro whose mother had been Julie's childhood Mammy. But neither Rad nor Reeve is interested in selling and they form an unprecedented black and white partnership to improve their land.

Although infuriated by the turn of events, Henry remains determined to push through the big land deal. And when Reeve's mother dies, Henry tries to persuade his wife to charge Reeve with illegal ownership of his property, confident that the bigoted Judge Purcell will rule against a Negro. Julie, however, decides to leave Henry because of his negligent care of their retarded son, and she withdraws her claim to Reeve's land.

In a desperate measure to force Rad and Reeve to sell, Henry dynamites the dam above their farms. As the area is flooded, Rad's oldest child is caught in the raging waters. Henry, whom the boy worshipped, attempts a rescue, but the child drowns. The tragedy brings Rad and Reeve even closer and they set about rebuilding their farms. As they do, they are joined by Negroes from all over the neighbouring countryside.

Preminger: I'm always looking for material. I read a lot. My organisation reads a lot. We get submissions of new novels. *Hurry Sundown* was sub-mitted eight months before it was published by an agent in manuscript form. I read the manuscript. It was very long, even longer than the novel, which as you know, is very long, and I was fascinated by the people. I was fascinated by the place, by the whole implication of the South in 1946 after World War Two which, in my opinion, was the starting point of the latest, let's say, civil rights movement. But this is not a picture about racial strife or civil rights. It's about people in the South, in the small city and the relationship between black and white to each other, and I think that what comes out in the film, if I do it right, is that the conditions, as dramatised, as shown, are the cause of all the things that happened between 1946 and 1966, in the last twenty years, be it civil legislation, riots, marches, even murders and acquittals. All that, I think, is visible in the relationships of these people in the small community in the South.

There is not a racial situation only in the South. As you know, the latest outbreaks happened in Los Angeles and Chicago, threatening in other places, in the Middle West and perhaps in New York, in Harlem, it is not only the South where the militant civil rights movement is at work. Pictures have been made about this, and I feel that whatever we do is quite obvious. We know where we stand.

The issues are quite clear. Nobody would expect me to make a film saying there should be equality of races, we know this, so I don't think this is very rewarding. I was interested to see the beginnings of all these things that happened, and why they happened, and to make a film about people, mainly, because I make films about people, after all, and about their community, and to show, without being too obvious, why the things that happened since have taken place.

I think the interesting thing about making films out of books is that I have a wealth of material to choose from. Naturally, I cannot possibly film all of a book like this, or do any book as a matter of fact, any novel, even if it is only four hundred pages. It is not possible to put on the screen every detail. I feel, and I told you all this even before the book was published, that this book is too long. I think the Gildens should have edited it, but it is their first book and first books usually are not edited, because people love their work. It is understandable, these two people worked on this book under great hardships for fourteen years, and they didn't want to shorten it. I don't use all the material in the book. They tell the whole life stories of almost every character. I have chosen in my opinion, six most interesting charac-

Jane Fonda with Michael Caine in HURRY SUNDOWN

ters and their story, Julie and Henry, played by Jane Fonda and Michael Caine, Vivian, played by Diahann Carroll, and Reeve, played by Robert Hook, who is a stage actor in New York, and Rad and Lulabelle played by Faye Dunawaye and by John Phillip Law, who just made a very big success in *The Russians Are Coming*. And all the characters, the smaller characters around them, who are necessary to their story, like Judge Purcell who my friend, Burgess Meredith, plays (the Penguin from the Batman) and his wife is played by Madeleine Sherwood, his daughter Sukie, a new young Southern actress called Donna Danton, and other people who belong to this community such as the Reverend Clem; but we don't go into his story like they do in the book, we only use him wherever he is necessary for the story of these main characters, and so it is possible to make a film out of a long book and not to tell the whole story.

I don't like to make statements about trying something different. I believe the greatest triumph of the director and of direction is not to be noticed. I don't look for any special camera angles. Actually, I always try a new approach and try certain new angles, but I am happiest if I can keep them my secrets.

With this picture, I have a clause that states that the picture cannot be shown on television without my written approval, so in this written approval I will put the conditions that they cannot interrupt it too often and they cannot cut it in any way, but as you know, so far, even to the highest court to which I appealed in the State of New York, I have lost my television suit about *Anatomy of a Murder*. It is inconceivable, but true.

CBC, Baton Rouge, La.,
November 1966.

The theme of *Hurry Sundown*, like *Advise and Consent* and *Anatomy of a Murder*, is part of American life. When I read the book, I felt that this particular time, the end of World War Two, was historically very important for the development of civil rights in America. The picture is not really about civil rights, though. This young farmer who comes back is certainly not a wild, liberal civil rights fighter. But, having been around with the Army in Europe, he has seen that all these prejudiced ideas he was brought up with about Negroes are wrong.

I think this is the general trend of what's happened during the last twenty years. Not so much the freedom fighter, the intellectual who comes from the East and marches, but a man who finally realises that his future does not depend on keeping Negroes down. So I deliberately didn't bring in anything of civil rights, no propaganda from the East or the North. I think that a character like the judge very much believes he's right. On the other hand, the sheriff is the same kind of character. You see, villains are too easy. This sheriff really likes Negroes. There is a line in the picture that I'm proud of. The sheriff tells this old Negro school teacher, who today would be called Uncle-Tomish, "I'll always be like a father to you people."

And this man of about seventy says to him, "I don't know, I haven't been in need of a Daddy for a long time."

SKIDOO. 1968. *Director:* Otto Preminger. *Original Screenplay:* Dorian Wm. Cannon. *Photography* (Panavision, Technicolor): Leon Shamroy. *Art Director:* Robert E. Smith. *Set Director:* Fred Price. *Special Effects:* Charles Spurgeon. *Editor:* George Rohrs. *Sound:* Glenn Anderson, Franklin Milton, Lloyd Hanks. *Assistant Director:* Eric von Stroheim Jr., Wally Jones, Al Murphey, Steven North. *Musical Director:* George Tipton. *Music and Lyrics:* Harry Nilsson. *Visual Consultant and Titles:* Sandy Dvore. *Choreography:* Tom Hansen. *Wardrobe Designer:* Rudi Gernreich. *Make-up:* Web Overlander. *Hairstyles:* Vivian Thompson. *Producer:* Otto Preminger. *Executive Assistant to the Producer:* Nat Rudich. *Production Managers:* C. Kenneth Deland, Howard Joslin. *Production:* Sigma Productions. *Release:* Paramount Pictures, December 2, 1968. 98 mins. *Players:* Jackie Gleason (*Tony Banks*), Carol Channing (*Flo Banks*), Groucho Marx ("*God*"), Frankie Avalon (*Angie*), Fred Clark (*A Tower Guard*), Michael Constantine (*Leech*), Frank Gorshin (*The Man*), John Philip Law (*Stash*), Peter Lawford (*The Senator*), Burgess Meredith (*The Warden*), George Raft (*Captain Garbaldo*), Cesar Romero (*Hechy*), Mickey Rooney ("*Blue Chips*" *Packard*), Austin Pendleton (*The Pro-*

Carol Channing, Jackie Gleason, Arnold Stang, John Phillip Law (on ground) and Alexandra Hay in SKIDOO

fessor [*Fred*]), Alexandra Hay (*Darlene Banks*), Luna ("*God's Mistress*), Arnold Stang (*Harry*), Doro Merande (*The Mayor*), Phil Arnold (*Her Husband*), Slim Pickens and Robert Donner (*Switchboard Operators*), Richard Kiel (*Beany*), Tom Law (*Geronimo*), Jaik Rosenstein ("*Eggs*" *Benedict*), Stacy King (*The Amazon*), Renny Roker and Roman Gabriel (*Prison Guards*), Harry Nilsson (*Tower Guard*), William Cannon (*Convict*), Themselves (*Stone Country*), Orange Country Ramblers (*Green Bay Packers*).

Story

Former mobster Tony Banks now operates a carwash and lives with his wife Flo in an affluent San Francisco suburb. His peaceful existence is disrupted when his teenage daughter Darlene falls in love with a long-haired hippy named Stash; two underworld cronies, Hechy and his son Angie, arrive with word that their gangland boss—"God"—wants Tony to do one last job by rubbing out "Blue Chips" Packard, an imprisoned mobster who is planning to tell all to a Senate Crime Committee in return for a life of luxurious solitary confinement.

At first Tony balks at "God's" suggestion, but later changes his mind when his best friend Harry is shot through the head. Once Tony's imprisonment has been arranged, Flo permits Stash and his flower friends to set up camp on the front lawn and take over the household.

While in jail, Tony comes in contact with some LSD-soaked stationery belonging to his draft-dodging cell-mate, the professor, and goes on an acid trip that convinces him that violence is evil. To avoid killing "Blue Chips," Tony and the Professor first get the entire prison high on LSD-spiked soup and then make a getaway in garbage cans attached to balloons made from plastic food bags.

As they make an aerial landing on "God's" yacht, where Darlene is being held prisoner, Flo and Stash arrive by water with a flotilla of hippies. Outwitted and outnumbered, "God" (dressed in hippie clothes) sails off on a raft with the Professor, as Tony is happily reunited with Flo, Darlene and Stash—his new son-in-law.

(The film opens with a biting satire on television programmes and commercials—Preminger's revenge for the cutting of his films on TV?—includes a weird, strange, effective "garbage can ballet," and ends with delightful singing titles and credits. **G.P.**)

Preminger (during the filming of Skidoo at Paramount Studios): I just came back from location in San Francisco. I have a very tricky set and it could only be done in the studio and these are the only few days we are going to shoot at the studio. I am not against studio shooting. Sometimes it is better and necessary to shoot at the studio, although I find that the way things are done at studios is obsolete and old-fashioned, the lighting, everything. It is strangely enough much faster today and much easier to shoot in real interiors also, not only exteriors, than in sets. I film practically everything in the real places. I really don't think it's a question of choice, it's what the director feels is the better way to do it. We are now going tomorrow into an abandoned jail where we're going to shoot in about three weeks all the sequences that take place in this jail, then we are going to San Pedro, and then we are going to shoot on a yacht, on the high seas and we have a balloon that we have constructed for this sequence. And all kinds of things in this little comedy.

I was working on the script for a picture that is based on a book by John Hersey called *Too Far To Walk*, but the script hasn't turned out right yet. A young writer called Bill Goodhart who had a big success with a play on Broadway called *Generation*, is working now on the final version, and instead of waiting until this is all finished, I found this story which amuses me and which I liked, and I make this film in the meantime. It's a comedy and I haven't done a comedy in a long time. A comedy like this, a kind of far-out, wild farce comedy is meaningless if explained. It is actually a confrontation of two groups of our society, the establishment and the so-called hippies, young people of this generation who rebel against the world as they found it and have developed their own philosophy of life.

The establishment, and that is the fun in it, is not represented by banks or by the government or civil service, or something like this, but it is represented by a former gangster who has now become respectable and is being called back into his organisation to perform a job for them and who, while

he's ready to kill people for his organisation, considers himself very respectable. But the young people who don't want anything from anybody, who just want to have their hair long and sing and play music and live a freer life, he considers them outcasts and it is interesting how eventually he is helped by one of them. It is a matter of attitudes in society. For once, it's an original screenplay. I actually found it through an agent sending me the screenplay to have one of his clients qualify to work on the other film. His name is Bill Cannon. And when I read it, I said I don't want him for the other film, but I'll buy this. So we worked on this story, improved it and then eventually I had somebody else also work on it, a man called Elliott Baker, who wrote a novel called *A Fine Madness* [*filmed by Irvin Kershner in 1966*— Ed.]'

Speaking of writers, their Guild would like to stop directors calling a film their own if they didn't write it. The whole issue is rather childish, but I'm not touched by it, because I have my own company and I give myself any credit I want to, and if the writers don't like it, they don't have to work for me; but what to me seems underhanded and wrong is that the Writers' Guild made an agreement, in their last contract, with the Motion Picture Producers' Association to for-

Carol Channing in SKIDOO

bid a so-called possessive credit for directors. Now, the fact that two organisations make a contract to deprive another organisation of a right they had since motion pictures began, and a right which is a matter of course for many directors, and a natural right all over Europe and in every other country, seems cheap. It is to me understandable (although I am not very active in Guild matters) that the Directors' Guild is trying to fight that. And the fight is very simple. They don't even go to Court. This writers' agreement lasts until 1970, or has been made until 1970. The directors, whose agreement is now expiring, say they won't negotiate with the Motion Picture Producers' Association, they will only negotiate with individual producers and if these producers have not signed with the writers, then they ask these producers for the right to give the directors possessive credits. It is childish, because I can think of twenty other credits to invent.

Alfred Hitchcock, who all his life has had his films called Alfred Hitchcock's *Psycho* and Alfred Hitchcock's . . ., contributes tremendously to the writing, even if he does not get writer's credit. It is not just like a play, where a writer writes a play, and submits it, and then a director is hired, and the play is being done as it was written, and the writer takes the risk—if the play is a flop, he makes no money. In our profession, the writer gets paid whether the picture is a success or not, and he sells his rights. He has no right to object and this is where the Writers' Guild is wrong. They should have told their writers, if you are powerful enough, then in your individual contract ask for the possessive credit for yourself, which has happened before. You can see it was Truman Capote's *In Cold Blood*, without any help from the Guild. Mr. Brooks, who even wrote the screenplay, had the right to possessive credit, but did not get it, so it's only a question of negotiations; but simply to make a blanket agreement, this is not the Union's, or Guild's, place. I think they are wrong, but I don't want to be involved in it, because I have really more interesting things to do than give speeches at Guilds.

Then we have the IATSE demands on the Government to stop so-called "runaway production" and tax films made abroad. I think they are also playing with very dangerous ideas, because films and particularly American films need the world market. They are an international mass medium of entertainment, of art or whatever you want to call it, and I think that if restrictions are put on people as to where they make their films, the next thing would be that these countries will not play our films, or that they will put taxes on our films, which will make it difficult to make any money with films that are produced here. In our world of free competition, all these things should be left alone.

Films are much more expensive made here, and I think that this could be at least partly remedied by the unions not insisting on unnecessarily large crews. When making a television film, the crew is about half the size of a film for the theatres. Why? It is the same kind of film we are making. You don't give, as it has turned out, people employment this way. You only chase people away. You cannot blame anybody who invests money in an enterprise, be it a film or anything else, if he produces it

cheaper somewhere else and he goes there. It is natural, our standard of living is higher, that costs are more expensive here, but on the other hand, in addition to it, the unions, in my opinion, are abusing their power by asking for too many people, by standing in the way of automation. We could have electronic lights, that are electronically controlled and have the cameras electronically controlled by remote control and save many people; but they just stop it, and I think in the long run they will have to learn that this is an international profession and people cannot be prevented from doing what is best for them.

Don't forget that the individuals who fight progress are usually business agents of these Guilds, who are voted in by members, who have to do a job for these people in order to keep their positions, to be voted in again, and they are not sincere. They know it is not a tenable position, but they are fighting, they are going to Congress, they're going to senators and, particularly now, before election time, they try to pass things. It's like censorship, it gets them a lot of publicity, but I don't think anything will happen. Until they change their outmoded practices, the situation will get worse. For example, I always keep my films open to so-called "observers." Because of union difficul-

F

ties, I cannot employ them and I cannot pay them. They cannot work, but they can observe and learn; I really don't think that film is something learned at the University. They have to learn certain basic principles, to see how a film is being made, and any young man who writes to me and has some qualifications is invited to come and watch. As long as he doesn't disturb, he's welcome.

CBC, Paramount Studios, Los Angeles, April 1968

After Skidoo *was finished :* I always plan a film in advance. I am not improvising (not that I belong to the school which feels a finished script is always essential). The picture was always planned as a comedy, as a wild comedy and the music was written in advance. I planned it like this. The *Dance of the Garbage Cans* was not impromptu either, I wanted to have a hallucinatory scene for these guards in order to explain how Gleason can escape out of the prison in a funny way, without making it a suspense drama. We staged this dance to the music and lyrics of the song, and then later on I used the process (which you may have seen at Expo '67) called "polarising." We took out all the normal natural colours, and then put in new colours, to emphasise this escape was taking place in the imagination of these two guards, who have been under the influence of LSD.

I took LSD in connection with this film. I took it only once and I've no desire to do it again. I did so after asking a doctor, who's probably the foremost expert on LSD, Doctor Sidney Cohen of New York, whether I should or not, and he told me that if I feel I'm reasonably balanced and not scared of it, that I could take it. What you saw in the film was really based on my experiences, I mean the physical symptoms that you see there, or what Gleason sees, are very much based on my "trip." I saw people very small. When the LSD started to work, I was in my home with my wife. She shrank, and she became very small. It is a very funny experience, but it is difficult to explain LSD. It is not the same feeling that comes after too many drinks or taking sedatives. It is the opposite. The brain nerves or brain cells are affected, they become sharper. It is as though I stood next to myself and while these hallucinations take place. I know all the time this is not reality. It was a very strange, amusing and central feeling to touch my skin. I still remember very clearly I had a more sensual feeling than I ever had before simply touching my hands one with the other. It's an amazing experience and I'm glad I did it, because I needed it for the film. I would not advise anybody to do it, until experiments have been more successful and more progress made in finding out what the possible damages are, what the doses are and who can and cannot take LSD.

I've talked to many young people and they all feel they have changed. The intelligent ones don't say necessarily that they have learned, that they have improved; but they feel they have learned something about their own character, their own desires, wishes and instincts which they didn't know before. I didn't feel that. My experience was mainly physical. Perhaps I'm too old, I mean I know myself too well. There's not much to learn any more. I would not play around with LSD. Young people must also consider there is a possibility that future generations could be influenced and deformed. I don't have any plans to have any more children, but I think a young man or a woman should really think twice before they take these drugs.

The outside scenes of the prison were Alcatraz in San Francisco. We shot most of the picture in real places, including the house of Gleason and his wife. Strange as it seems, even the furniture belonged in this house. Everything I found in San Francisco. The interior of the prison I shot in an abandoned prison in Los Angeles, downtown. I feel that wher-ever possible, even in a comedy like this, it gives a feeling of reality to work in real sets than in studio built sets. There was only one set, the apartment of Frankie Avalon, because all these electronic devices and changes had to be built.

Regarding the singing credits at the end, it is very frustrating for a director, when he has the credits at the end, to see the audience walk out. They walk out because (let's be honest) the public is interested only perhaps in who played the parts, the stars and the actors, and perhaps the director and the writer. But then when they go on and give credit to all the technicians, who wants to know who was the chief electrician except the chief electrician himself, who likes to read his name, and his family who wants to read his name? I was sitting in my office one day with a composer, who is a very talented young man, and had all this list of names before me, and I felt very bad about it. I said to him "How would it be if we wrote a song with these names?" He started to "ad lib" right there, and we did it. Then a young, new designer worded the titles visually for me, and it turned out very well, I think. Nobody leaves. I say "stop," freeze the frame, and then it becomes quite an amusing ending.

CBC, Park Plaza Hotel,
Toronto, December 1968

Preminger on the film: I don't think many people *adore* it. Except my wife, who adores all my pictures, because that's what you get married for. I do believe that the picture has some funny things in it, and some interesting things. But, if you ask me my honest opinion, I don't think it was altogether successful in projecting what I wanted to project.

Maybe one of the faults was that while I worked very well with Gleason, while he's a very professional actor, there was still a kind of wall between us.

Now, while I could not argue with Gleason about what he was doing—it was all *correct*—there is such a difference between us, in the texture of our characters (and if he should read this he would probably say he's very happy about the difference). There is a different attitude toward life, toward our profession, toward man, toward woman, toward friendship, toward love, toward war, toward peace, toward politics—toward *everything*. It made it impossible to project the meaning which I felt lay underneath the comedy. That's why for me the picture is not really successful.

TELL ME THAT YOU LOVE ME, JUNIE MOON. 1970. *Director :* Otto Preminger. *Screenplay :* Marjorie Kellogg. *Based on her own novel.* *Photography* (Technicolor): Boris Kaufman. *Set Director :* Morris Hoffman. *Editors :* Henry Berman, Dean O. Ball. *Sound :* Ben Winkler, Franklin Milton, Stanley Gordon. *Assistant Director :* Norman Cook. *Music :* Philip Springer. *Lyrics for* "The Rake," "Work Your Show" *by :* Estelle Levitt. *Lyrics and Music for* "Old Devil Time" *by :* Pete Seeger. "Elvira" *music and lyrics by :* Pacific Gas and Electric. *Music Editor :* Robert Tracy. *Titles :* Stanley Cortez, Howard A. Anderson Co. *Sound Effects :* Edit-Rite Inc. *Script Supervisors :* Wallace Bennett, Cleo Anton. *Costume Co-ordinator :* Hope Bryce. *Wardrobe Designers :* Ron Talsky, Phyllis Garr. *Make-up :* Charles Schram. *Producer :* Otto Preminger. *Associate Producer :* Nat Rudich. *Executive Assistant to the Producer :* Erik Kirkland. *Production Manager :* Robert Vreeland. *Production :* Sigma Films. *Release :* Paramount Pictures, May 11, 1970. 112 mins. (Official U.S. entry at Cannes 1970.) *Players :* Liza Minnelli (*Junie Moon*), Ken Howard (*Arthur*), Robert Moore (*Warren*), James Coco (*Mario*), Kay Thompson (*Gregory*), Fred Williamson (*Beach Boy*), Ben Piazza (*Jesse*), Emily Yancy (*Solana*), Leonard Frey (*Guiles*), Clarice Taylor (*Minnie*), James Beard (*Sidney Wyner*), Julie Bovasso (*Ramona*), Gina Collins (*Lila*), Barbara Logan (*Mother*

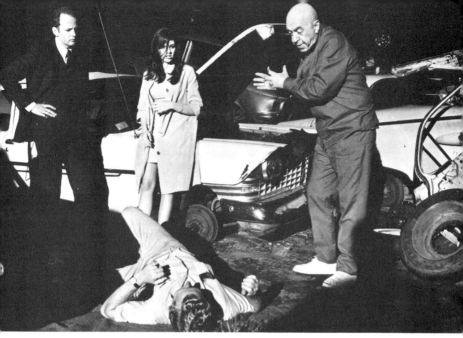

Preminger directing the cemetery sequence in TELL ME THAT YOU LOVE ME, JUNIE MOON

Moon), Nancy Marchand (*Nurse Oxford*), Lynn Milgrim (*Nurse Holt*), Ric O. Feldman (*Joebee*), James D. Pasternak (*The Artist*), Angelique Pettyjohn (*Melissa*), Anne Revere (*Miss Farber*), Elaine Shore (*Mr. Wyner*), Guy Sorel (*Dr. Gaines*), Wayne Tippett (*Dr. Miller*), Pacific Gas & Electric (*Themselves*) and Pete Seeger singing "Old Devil Time."

Story

"Once there were three patients who met in the hospital and decided to live together. They arrived at this decision because they had no place to go when they were discharged. Despite the fact that these patients often quarrelled and nagged each other, and had, so far as they knew, nothing in common, they formed an odd balance—like three pawnshop balls . . ." (from *Tell Me*

That You Love Me, Junie Moon by Marjorie Kellogg).

Preminger: I did the screenplay together with Miss Marjorie Kellogg. It is her first screenplay and there are hardly any changes. The characters remained intact, and the theme and I think, if you like the book, you should also like the film. We started in California, looking for a small town. The book doesn't give any definite location, but we couldn't find any small town in California that had the charm and the real character of small towns as we think of them. They have become so commercialised, they have all the same neon signs, they don't look photographically like a small town, so we moved to Canada. We were in Quebec province. We found some locations, but then there were difficulties about unions, which were not entirely due to Canada. They were also due to the United States unions with whom we have contracts, and we then came here to New England and found this little town here, Manchester, and some other places which seemed to be very right for the film.

I have quite an interesting cast. I have Liza Minnelli, who has done two films before, one *Charlie Bubbles*, and one that hasn't been released yet, called *The Sterile Cuckoo* and she plays the lead. I selected her, she was my first choice. I think she is giving a remarkable performance, and will move with this picture into the front rank of actors and stars. During this film she experienced the tragic death of her mother, and the way she behaved during these trying days, and took care of all the arrangements, was really an inspiration to watch. I hope she will be happy, happier than her mother who, as you know, was very talented, too, but led a very tragic life. Then I met a young man called Ken Howard, whom I saw at the opening of a musical, *1776*; he played Thomas Jefferson. I made a test with him, and I think he's an exceptional young man. The second part is played by a director, Robert Moore. This young director did the two most successful plays in New York, off Broadway, *Boys in the Band*, and on Broadway, *Promises, Promises*, this past year. He came to see me and said he would like to play a small part because he would like to observe film-making, in order some time to direct films himself. As we talked, I found him very interesting and thought he would be very good for the third lead. I offered him this, I said "Let's make a test, and if you like the test, you'll play the part." So he plays the third starring part. He had given Ken Howard his first job in *Promises, Promises*, a small part when he came out of Yale Drama School. Then he met on the set the man who plays the fish store owner, James Coco, and they had already previously made an agreement to do *The Last of the Red Hot Lovers*. We became all one small family and the making of the film was a really warm, human experience. So you see, the cast is from the New York stage, more than from the screen.

The gratifying thing was that these three actors became friends, very much like the characters in the book, as in the film; like the parts they played, and this friendship helped me very much in making the film, because they really lived the story. They worked it out, and I hope (I cannot judge) this shows on the screen. We felt during the making of the film such friendship for each other that there was really never a problem that couldn't be solved.

Tomorrow I must be in Court in Quincy, Massachusetts. You see, I filmed the scene of *Junie Moon* undressing for the strange man in a cemetery. The reason I did so was because I wanted to be private to have complete control, without photographers shooting from windows. The police closed the cemetery. Everybody knew about my shooting there. Nobody said it was wrong. The man who owned the cemetery made a contract with me. I paid him a hundred dollars for shooting there, and I even went to his

mother's birthday party. Later, a woman wrote to me saying I had desecrated her husband's grave and she implied that perhaps a thousand dollars or so would heal her wounds. I might have given in to this blackmail, when I got another letter which was funnier. A man wrote me saying he owned several plots in this cemetery which he meant to resell and that the publicity about my shooting there had depressed the real estate values, and he wanted money too. I felt if I gave in to one, it would be endless, so I said "no." The woman went to her lawyer, who found out there was an old statute in Massachusetts, I think 1887, or so, which said that anybody who creates a nuisance in a graveyard is subject to a fine between one and one hundred dollars. It's a misdemeanour. So I told my lawyer "Why don't you pay them a hundred dollars and let me go?" But the judge, who apparently is a movie fan, decided that I must be there. He postponed it and postponed it and finally I was served when I went for a press luncheon to Boston, and now (a week from today) it will finally finish. We were very careful, no names are visible, and as a matter of fact, I got a very charming letter from a lady who is a doctor, and a widow of a doctor. She wrote to me and said "I don't want you to use my name, because I live in Quincy and I

Liza Minnelli with Ken Howard in
TELL ME THAT YOU LOVE ME,
JUNIE MOON

have to work there. My husband is also buried in the cemetery and I don't mind that you made the film there; but what I do mind is that every week people steal all the bronze and metal fittings from all the graves. Why don't they publicise that, instead of protesting your film?" Anyway, I cannot go to jail. A hundred dollars is the maximum fine. [*Preminger was found not guilty of desecrating the cemetery.*]

This is not a film made for "today's audience." I don't make movies thinking of audiences, of today or yesterday or tomorrow. I feel, for better or for worse, that I live today,

and I think that all this talk about youth market and young people and old people, this is all too much of a generalisation to be true. The great word is "youth-oriented." We were always youth-oriented, did anybody ever throw young people out of theatres? Young people have always been more interested in movies. At the opening of *Junie Moon* last night, people were standing in line, and I looked at them. There was hardly anybody over twenty-five, not even thirty. They were all young people. I have very many things in common with young people and often with older people. It depends on individuals, not on young and old, and I can only make a movie if I personally get excited, enthusiastic about a story, a theme, about characters, and I hope then if I re-create them in my medium, that other people will be interested and excited and enthusiastic about them, and sometimes I'm right and sometimes I'm wrong. That's success or failure. But I mean I cannot think in terms: what am I going to do, to calculate, if I put a few parts of violence and a little sex and a little this and that in, that it will please people. I don't think it's possible, and the best proof is that imitations never work. A studio has one surprise success with a film called *The Sound of Music* and then everyone imitates it. Now, a picture came out, a small picture, *Easy Rider*. Now everybody tries to do *Easy Rider*'s. The fact is that making pictures is not like making automobiles or shoes, mass production. That is why I really hate the word "industry," which people use so often. It is a single effort done by a man, or woman, with a team and it's an individual creation and if possible, original, new and unique, not an imitation of something else. Now you cannot ensure success by saying "because this thing was successful, I'm going to imitate it." It never works. But in spite of all the bad experiences, in our profession people always try to do this again. They never stop. They never learn. That's their problem.

I think eventually the producer will carry out his own distribution because the older companies are no longer dependable. They change so often, like governments in South American states. Every couple of years, they have a revolution. At some studios, in fact, every couple of months there's a new government and they make practically the same statements about youth, about costs, about changing trends, they throw away half their old films, because the more loss they show, before they came in, the more successful they seem when they start. In other words, if on taking over a movie company, the new man makes a statement saying: "Last year the movie company lost thirty million dollars" and after the first year of his *régime*, he announces "we lost only fifteen million dollars!" it's counted as a profit of fifteen million! The people who write that everything should be for young people are usually elderly men and women. Now why don't they retire? I am a pretty old man and I'm very happy about it. I only hope I can be old a long, long time because I want to live long and work long. Age doesn't bother me at all. Sometimes I feel younger on Friday in the week than on Monday. I go backwards.

I am working now with two talented

Ken Howard, Liza Minnelli and Robert Moore in TELL ME THAT YOU LOVE ME, JUNIE MOON

writers on a film called *Such Good Friends*. It's a novel by a young writer, again a woman (I'm practically working for the women's liberation front!) One of the writers is also a woman who has just also had a novel out called *Play It Where It Lays*. Her name is Joan Bidyon. Maybe you saw it, and her husband John Gregory Dunne wrote a book called *The Studio*. I worked practically eight, ten hours a day on this script with them. I am also reading other stories for future productions and trying to do a play on Broadway. So I don't worry which one is my best or most satisfactory picture.

I had a contest going on during production to encourage new filmmakers to make a short film about the film-making, a behind the scenes movie. There are ten young filmmakers working on that and I can hardly wait to see the results. The first prize is a thousand dollars, second and third prize five hundred dollars each.

CBC, October 1970

Some Questions from Preminger's Press Conference at Cannes 1970 after the projection:

PREMINGER: The gentleman asked if the chanson was in the script, the Pete Seeger song, and I explained "No," that when I finished the picture, I showed the film to Mr. Seeger who is a famous American composer and folk singer, and asked him to create a song to help the mood, to set the mood for the picture, and deliberately not to refer either to the film or to the characters. It would have been very easy to write a song, "Tell Me That You Love Me, Junie Moon," but I thought we have had enough of title songs, so we decided on a song which was completely separate from the film, only in the same mood.

PREMINGER: It is not epilepsy, it is an undiagnosed illness. If you listen to the dialogue, you will find that it says this. Arthur makes fun of it, because the hospital doesn't know what it is. They told him to put his right finger and his left finger to the nose to try . . . but they never found out what was wrong, and they don't find it to the end. I just bought a new book which shows even less aptitude on the part of the medical profession, where a man dies because he's allergic to an anaesthetic. It's called *Such Good Friends*. And this book is based on the real case of a newspaper man, the husband of the author, who died like this. The doctors didn't even question to see if he's allergic to this anaesthetic. There are many things happening in medicine, unfortunately, that cannot be explained. The medical facts in *Junie Moon* I can defend, because they were checked by doctors. There are cases where people act exactly like this young man and the doctors cannot diagnose what is wrong with him. Traduisez!

PREMINGER: Have I ever *not* worked on the editing of my film? Now, you see, the editing. It's a great fallacy, you often read in reviews: "it was brilliantly edited by so-and-so." The editing is really part of the director's job. The director tells the editor exactly what to use and what not to use. It is never an editor who edits the film. An editor or cutter is like the right arm. Naturally, if he is sensitive, he's doing a better job and understands the director better, he makes suggestions. Editing is just as important as the rehearsing with the actors or the working on the script. The director's job is first to work on the script with the writers and direct them, then work with the art director on the selection of locations and the building of sets, then work with the casting director on the casting. He makes the final decisions, nobody else, then works with the actors, then eventually works with the editor, and eventually corrects the colour prints, if he finds them. That is the most difficult thing, because unfortunately in our very technological society, where perfection should be a matter of course, there is tremendous sloppiness about prints, about projection. Normally when you go to a theatre,

most of the time they're playing films out of focus, and the sound is distorted. It's unbelievable that people go to movies still, when you consider what the exhibitor does (the sins and crimes of the exhibitors) and when you talk to them, then they say that if the movie is good, it doesn't matter. Sadly, this is true, in a way, but still . . . I mean it's just like wearing dirty shirts. People should do it as well as they can, be perfect, try to get perfection in technical things, which is easy, because it has nothing to do with invention or talent. It can be done, but exhibitors don't want to hear that.

QUESTION: To what extent do you consider the fact that more people will probably see your film on television than in a theatre?

PREMINGER: No, I don't think about these things because I would commit suicide.

QUESTION: Do you find a balance between vulgarity and sentiment?

PREMINGER: This is a question of taste I cannot decide. I mean you're asking me to write a review about my own film. (*LAUGHTER*) Maybe I don't find a balance between vulgarity and sentiment. I mean that is up for you to judge. I hope I am not vulgar, and I don't do anything vulgar, but who knows what you think?

Script Extract from SUCH GOOD FRIENDS

INT. JULIE'S CLOSET. LATE AFTERNOON.

The screen is black. We can hear the sound of children's
voices and the sharp voice of an adult. A phone is ringing
somewhere. There is a sudden spill of light on to the
screen. It widens until we see that we are in the interior
of a closet. JULIE MESSINGER is framed in the doorway.
There is a large roller in her hair and a strip of Scotch
tape across her bangs. She rifles quickly through the
clothes, grabs a hanger with a pair of slacks on it and
closes the door as a female voice (DARLENE) calls, "Mrs.
Messinger."

INT. MESSINGER BEDROOM. LATE AFTERNOON.

The bedroom is large, thickly carpeted. well furnished
and vaguely disorganized. A box lies on the bed, there is
a pair of shoes and a matching purse standing on the dresser,
a coloring book and a pile of crayons on the floor, and a vase
with two dried out ferns stands in front of the window. Julie
Messinger is around twenty-nine. She is dressed in a bras-
siere and panty hose. As Darlene continues to call, "Mrs.
Messinger" from off screen, she begins frantically pulling
on the slacks.

> DARLENE
> (Off screen)
> Mrs. Messinger! Phone. Mrs.
> Messinger?

> JULIE
> (Struggling to close
> the zipper)
> I can't talk now, Darlene. Can
> you ask who's calling and tell
> them I'll call back.

She whips on her shoes, opens the box on the bed, and lifts
out a vest that is an open lattice work of tiny pearls strung
together loosely with two satin shoe strings to tie it together
across the midriff.

> DARLENE
> (Off screen)
> It's Doctor Spector. He wan's
> to talk to you.

(CONTINUED) EM-A

172

Script Extract from *SUCH GOOD FRIENDS*

FANTASY: FULL SHOT. RICHARD, FITCH, KALMAN, JULIE.

Kalman reaches over, and tweaks one of her breasts.. then removes a pair of scissors from his pocket, cuts the vest ties and rips off the vest.

> KALMAN (Cont.)
> (the real one, off screen)
> ..but I felt it was, it is, a duty of the artist to try and influence his time--if he can. And even though I disapprove of the President's policies...

FANTASY. JULIE

She is looking at her now naked breasts and, as she looks down, her eyes widen in surprise.

> KALMAN (Cont.)
> (the real one, off screen)
> ...every bit as much as Robert Lowell, it is my belief that...

FANTASY. KALMAN. JULIE'S POV.

Kalman's legs are bare. As she looks up, she (and we) sees that he is completely nude except for a copy of his book which he holds in front of his crotch and his red carnation which is now pinned to his skin in the same position where it once was pinned to his jacket.

> KALMAN (Cont.)
> (the real one, off screen)
> ..if I could just got to the White House as a spokesman for the artists of this startled nation...
> (the fantasy one who speaks as soon as the POV camera reaches his face)
> and say to the President, how about a little nookie?...

FULL SHOT. RICHARD, FITCH, KALMAN, JULIE.

They are as before. Kalman and Julie are clothed. Kalman is still talking. Julie wears the same interested expression.

> KALMAN
> I would have performed a valuable service for this troubled land.

> RICHARD
> I read your speech in the Times. I thought it was a very important speech.

> (CONTINUED) EM-A

BUNNY LAKE
IS MISSING

AN OTTO PREMINGER FILM

Logo for BUNNY LAKE, designed by Saul Bass & Associates

Conclusions

Many directors have all wanted in a sense to have complete freedom, and they talk about wanting to follow a picture right through so that when they have finished their film they would also have something to say about the way it is advertised, and what the advertising looks like in the theatres and everything else. Few of them do it, because going through all this is sometimes onerous and difficult. I think it is very interesting and important, part of being a film-maker. I like it and I do it. Some people say "Well, that doesn't have much to do with the art of making the film." I don't like to use the word "art" anyway, and I think everything is part of the art. I have a painting downstairs, a very big painting by Miro, and he himself made a frame for this painting out of the ceiling of a Spanish country house. The frames of my other paintings are very simple, but I kept this frame because he felt this frame was an important part of his painting. The same is true about the publicity, the way a picture is presented—that is all part of it, I think it is important and whatever I can contribute to it, I'll do, even going to other countries. I am very violently against the division between American and foreign pictures. Pictures, like anything even slightly related to art, are international. I don't feel you are a foreigner and I hope you don't feel that I am a foreigner to you. There are many other things that make people feel compatible, or akin, than where they were born, what language they speak.

I don't worry about my "directing style." It's very easy to set the camera up, to obtain strange angles, but that is not style. Whether or not I have a style will probably be decided by people like you, who are interested in films, directors, and picture-makers; and maybe after I am dead, and someone has the time, he will look at all my films together and will find out there is something there—that is style. There was a director (I don't want to mention his name) when I was at Fox who used to dig deep holes in the floor where the stage is so that he could shoot up with his camera. He forgot that if he put his sets on a platform it would have been easier. That is not style, it is phony, people who use old tricks. Sometimes it is interesting to shoot a scene out of focus as I did in *Junie Moon*, and to use deliberately a Cinema-Scope lens without unsqueezing it, or to divide the screen, the expanse; but to think this is style is wrong. If the story calls for tricks like this, to use them is one thing; but the style is really in the whole work of a man, in his attitude, rather than in external things. It is the attitude towards life, characters, people, the whole universe, that creates style in a man's work, whether he is a motion picture maker, a painter, or a musician, or a writer, that's the style. Some poets do not use any capital letters, and write everything in lower case; that's not style. I think you cannot look at the paintings of Picasso without recognising Picasso, although he has seventeen "styles." They were all at various times different and still the same hand. That is true in a smaller way, maybe, about motion picture makers, and if people will discover it after I have gone, I will probably be very happy about it, wherever I am. If they don't, I will also, I hope, be happy wherever I am. I'm not going to worry about it.

Critics and criticism? It is always nicer to get good reviews, but basically I know very few critics with whom I agree when I read them, which I don't always do. I think they are mainly a problem for their readers, their newspapers and magazines, not my problem. I prefer to have people say or write nice things, but if they don't, I'll be damned if I'll spend one sleepless hour about it! I wouldn't say they have no function. Everything, whether it's a critic, a festival or a motion picture magazine, everything that heightens interest in films is important—whether it's negative or positive. Eventually, critics who always tear everything down lose their readers, because their readers might find out that they like things these critics don't like. But the very fact that today—it didn't happen in the beginning of films—newspapers and magazines devote a lot of space to criticism of films, to writing about films, makes films a more important medium, or television, which I consider part of films of the future.

It's important that people talk about us, and think about us. It cannot always be flattering. I might see a picture when I'm cutting it

176

Etienne Girardot, Jack Haley, Ann Sothern, Walter Catlett, John Carradine, and Mary Boland in DANGER, LOVE AT WORK

maybe three hundred times, but then the first time, or the second time with an audience, it's a new film. That's why it is so criminal that most critics refuse to see films in theatres, that most critics insist on seeing it by themselves or with two or three people in the projection room. It's not the same film.

I have been described as the director who acts like a producer. In essence the titles don't matter. If there is a different man directing, a different man producing, the stronger personality will prevail, and his influence, which is felt, is the more important. If you produce and direct then this doesn't arise, and there are no conflicts. You know who's making the film. People have come to realise, and to appreciate that the director from the beginning to the end really forms the film. I work to a method, not to a formula. I find myself attracted to themes of the present day more than stories of the past. I live in the Twentieth century and I am interested in what goes on around me. My interests do change; but what I try quite deliberately to do is to avoid any set formula, to avoid making one picture after another of the same kind. After *Laura*, a suspense story, it was very tempting because the picture was a success and everybody used to send me all their suspense stories. But I try to have as much diversification as possible.

I don't work fast. But I think I have organised myself to a point where I don't do anything unnecessary. I think that most delays in pictures come from a certain insecurity or from a feeling that "I can do it two ways and then decide." I try to decide in advance when I am working with the writer on the script, I only change the script when it is too long, which unfortunately it often tends to be. Then I try to cut and not to do unnecessary scenes which I shall not be able to use. But I don't work faster than anyone else; on the contrary, once on the stage I try to give everybody the feeling that they have all the time in the world, although I know they don't because time when filming is a very expensive commodity. I work mainly from novels because there is so much rich material readily available in interesting books that I have no inhibitions about buying them. They may only serve as a useful point of departure. (I would film an original screenplay if I thought it suitable.) I don't have books "adapted." I don't "illustrate" novels. I re-create them for the screen as I would re-create an original story with a writer. I work with the writers, so there is already no formula.

In everything there is a certain time order. First I have to write the script and then I start to shoot; as far as that goes there is a method, but there is no method or formula in how I arrive at the end of creation. Sometimes I let one writer do it, sometimes there are four working with me until the script is right in my opinion. The only rule is that I go by my own instincts, and when I say instincts, I *mean* instincts. I am not an analytical man—I do things the way I feel them, by instincts, by impulse. Film is part of my life, and just as life or a period of life goes by and becomes part of the past, a film, as much as I enjoy doing it, working on it, being completely immersed in it—all I think and feel and work about—when I finish it, it's gone, it's past—like everything. It's sad, but there is satisfaction in knowing I have a chance to go on, and to go further. This is the main thing about films: once a film is finished, I detach myself from it and I think and work on the future film. I am thinking now during these days— you probably don't notice it even if you are there and watch me—

Charles Bickford, Gene Tierney, and Richard Conte in WHIRLPOOL

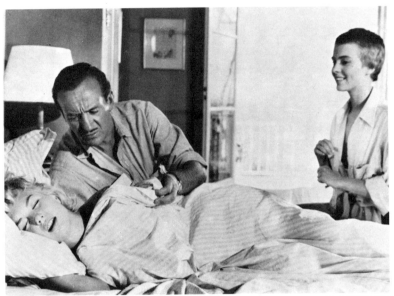

Mylène Demongeot, David Niven and Jean Seberg in BONJOUR
TRISTESSE

much more about the next film, the next two films, that I am embark-
ing on, than about *Junie Moon*. I am doing what is necessary for *Junie
Moon* because, as I told you, I think this part of my work as a picture-
maker, producer, to see that the films get the best possible treatment,
get to the people, because you make pictures for people. Still, that is
not as interesting as the fact that I am now working on two more
stories, I am thinking about the casting, the writing, when I'll do
them, and which I'll do first. That fills my thoughts all day.

Many times I have been described as a controversial film-maker.
I don't know what it means! I never do things deliberately to create
controversy or news. On the other hand, controversy is not bad.

People only talk or argue about subjects or people who are interesting. So I am not worried about being called controversial. Because film is not alive completely, because what you do is fixed permanently you must be precise. Changing a few lines or positions on the stage doesn't matter because there is a compact between the actor and the audience, and the performance will take place again tomorrow. People feel an actor has made a mistake and they correct it right there. In film there are no compensating factors. Mistakes go into a translation, into subtitles, into dubbing, because this is the final script which is used as the basis for that. If a thing is wrong, it is not corrected. If it is mechanically wrong, then it stays wrong, and that's why you have to be more

Dana Andrews and Gene Tierney in WHERE THE SIDEWALK ENDS

precise in every way. There is never a first time for a director to see his film complete, because during the stages of editing, sound recording and scoring, I see and direct it constantly. I am there when they are putting the music on, and I say when I want another take—it is too loud, that is too low—and when they mix the sound—and so it cannot appear fresh or new, but something is added when I see it for the first time after all this with an audience. An audience is a strange mystery in show business. The audience, sometimes quiet, sometimes responsive, adds the missing element. That is very exciting to me, the first time, or the first few times when I see it with an audience.

I have told you what I think of censorship. Since then the M.P.P.A. has established a voluntary system of ratings for motion pictures. I am not opposed to it as long as it is voluntary. I think there is a lot of bureaucracy about it and I hope it works, but you see, these schemes happen because some people in big companies (it should really not be called producers, but distributors' association) are always scared of censorship. I believe that if censorship is threatened, they should fight it because in the United States of America, according to the constitution, there can be no censorship and I have won and other people have won whenever we fought it. These classifications are intended to be nothing else than a warning sign for parents as to the suitability of certain movies for their children. We'll see what happens. It is up to the parents. If parents don't give their children a careful education, films or no films, they'll end up in a bad way. It is certainly not up to us to police children or to educate them. I also believe that children who are given by their parents, or by their educators, by their schools, the solid standard of what is good or bad, what is right or wrong, are not in much danger when they see a sexy scene or even a violent scene; although I am more against violence than against sex, but this is a personal matter.

For the cameraman, everything is mathematics in photography. He can help me with the mood, if I tell him what mood this particular scene should have, and if I tell him about my ideas, what I want, how I would like it darker, realistic or glossy, but the set-ups you see on the screen are determined by the director. In other words, the French, who have this *auteur* theory, are really right. The medium *is* a director's medium and many directors (I don't do it, I have everything on paper before I start and I rarely change it) now shoot without a script and then it is their film. That is the way film is. It is not a medium of committees, it is one man's medium. That's why the film made a tremendous step forward when it escaped the bureaucracy, or whatever you want to call it, of the major studios, from "the boss" who had the final word in cutting, the script and the casting. Even during that time the successful director did not have to ask for permission for everything. It was only difficult until the first success. Then Mr. Zanuck or Mr. Louis B. Mayer needed the director and did not interfere, even if the contract provided that they had the last word in cutting, in editing. They didn't interfere as much as people thought they did. The difficulties arose when you wanted to try something different.

I sometimes wonder what happens to all of the people I have worked with. A man who used to own the house next door, Ilya Lopert, said something very wise one day.

He was at the funeral of a film executive (he is a distributor, works with United Artists) and he said : "I suddenly realised that I know more dead people than live people." It becomes true. We go through life and do not realise it because we go on living, and unless it affects us very closely, we accept that people die. Then comes the realisation that one more person has gone ; it is natural as we grow older. It is another fact I have learned to live with. I very early told myself that death is part of life, that it is inevitable, and that makes it so much more important to do, while I can, all the things I want to do, to enjoy life. You will find, if you watch me, that I basically enjoy life. It is actually not my business to look at contracts, law suits, but I do it because it has to be done, and I don't let it weigh me down, I think of other things, and I work on other things—and it works.

Ralph Ballamy and Gary Cooper in THE COURT MARTIAL OF
BILLY MITCHELL

Over a long life like mine certain people have left an impression and I remember them for ever. As I talk—I don't think about it often—I feel, for instance, that my experience with Laurette Taylor, or with Roosevelt, with Jack Barrymore, with a man like Gary Cooper (who was also a wonderful actor, he knew always what he wanted to do) or with Charles Laughton through his illness—different experiences, but all so worthwhile. And there are so many other people! The satisfactions are not only that I like my work, but that it brings me in contact with all kinds of people. In spite of all the conflicts that I had with Zanuck (and I don't see him often now though we live here), I have great regard for him. In his way, he is also a remarkable man,

Liza Minnelli in TELL ME THAT YOU LOVE ME, JUNIE
MOON

a professional man. In our profession it is regrettable that now with
the take-over of motion pictures by businessmen, these people, who
might be very clever in their own right, are not showmen. Take a man
like Harry Cohn. He was certainly not well educated, nor was he a
saint, or a gentleman, but he was a great showman. We could talk to
him because he was a personality, he was fun to be with. David
Merrick today is a great showman. But when businessmen take over a
company, and are more impressed by the fact that they have starlets
who they feel they can go to bed with (they deserve to be called silly
little people) then I think motion pictures are bound to suffer.

I still think the cutting of films for television is deplorable. I think it is fraud to distribute a film under the name *Anatomy of a Murder*, and then to permit 105 different television stations to cut it the way they like because they need time for commercials. If the owner of the TV station shows *Anatomy of a Murder*, it should be the *Anatomy of a Murder* that I made, and the way I showed it in theatres should be the way it is shown everywhere. It's as simple as that, down to earth and unpretentious! And I hope in time it will come about. Soon there will be a tremendous difference, and people will have big TV screens in rooms. When I show 16 mm I have a lens to make the picture as big as 35 mm. So it will be with television. Perhaps new films will be shown first on television. Don't forget that a few years ago it was difficult to buy even an 8 mm camera. Today you buy a Super-8 camera and without focusing it works properly. All this is a question of technical accomplishment, and advances. They will come soon, they will help film-makers to tell stories as long as we don't get too much involved in the technique. Don't forget that the essential factor is not technique but *what* we want to tell and *what* we want to do, and *how* we want to present it in order to involve audiences in matters of consequence, in patterns of human behaviour.

With the freedom I have today to choose any theme or subject, and the opportunities to learn about people and events, and the possibilities of revealing life in its many forms to audiences everywhere, I find my work continuously fascinating and a constant challenge; and believe me, there is a challenge every ten minutes. This is why I would rather make motion pictures than do anything else in life.

Preminger on His Acting

I gave up acting when I was nineteen. Then I came here and I wanted only to direct. I have told you how I came to play the Nazi in the play, *Margin for Error*. The role in *The Pied Piper* (1942) was a direct outcome of being seen on the stage by Nunnally Johnson, who wrote this. I was then asked to play the heavy in Sam Goldwyn's *They Got Me Covered* (1942) and then I repeated my stage role in the film of *Margin for Error* (1943). Many of us at Fox appeared in *Where Do We Go from Here* (1945) because we were friends with Gregory Ratoff, who directed it. I didn't act again until 1953 when my friend, Billy Wilder, asked me to be the Nazi in *Stalag 17*. In 1963 I agreed to play an English butler (imagine me as an English butler!) for another friend, Alexander Paal, in his film *Millie Goes to Budapest*, shot in London, which I did. Then they went to Budapest and shot it all again, but I had not the time to go there and play the part again. So I do not know where my scenes are from the original.

My last appearance on the screen was as Mr. Freeze in *Batman*. And here is a story: I have twins who are going to be ten years in three weeks. Three years ago, I think it was, they used to watch *Batman* every Wednesday and Thursday on television and the producer of *Batman*, Bill Dozier, is a friend of mine. When he said to me, "Why don't you play one of the heavies?" (which I normally would never have done) "Play Mr. Freeze in *Batman*!" I said it would be a wonderful surprise and wonderful to watch my children when they turn on this programme and suddenly see me there. And it was wonderful and they became very famous in school, and I must tell you, there was really something very funny in connection with this. They go to a French school in New York, because we travel a lot and this school has branches everywhere in the world, in London, in Paris, in Los Angeles, in Rome, and there are very many children of ambassadors to the United Nations there, and one of their friends called Boday was an African boy, whose father was an ambassador from Guinea or some place (he's in the meantime been recalled and probably shot).

When my children spread the word in school about me playing Mr. Freeze in *Batman*, Boday told them, "My father is standing by, and as soon as a part is available, he will also be in *Batman*."

Preminger's Stage Productions

In Austria

1925 **KREIDERKREIS** [**Chalk Circle**]
Written by: Klabund. Based on the same Chinese legend as the play by Brecht *The Caucasian Chalk Circle*.

1931 **VORUNTERSUCHUNG** [**Preliminary Inquiry**]
5 acts. Written by: Max Alsberg and Otto Ernst Hesse. World *première*: January 20, 1931. 113 performances, Josefstadt Theatre, Vienna. *Preminger's first great success. (Filmed the same year by Robert Siodmak and Henri Chomette.)*

1931 **REPORTER** [**Front Page**]
3 scenes. Written by: Ben Hecht and Charles McArthur. Translated by: R. Lothar. *Première*: June 9, 1931. 23 performances, Josefstadt Theatre, Vienna.

1933 **DIE LIEBE DES JUNGEN NOSTY** [**The Love of Young Nosty**]
3 acts. Written by: Koloman von Mikszath. *Première*: September 22, 1933. 55 performances.

1933 **MAKART**
5 acts. Written by: Duchinsky. *Première*: November 10, 1933. 18 performances.

1934 **MEHR ALS LIEBE** [**More than Love**]
3 acts. Written by: L. Bus Fekete. *Première*: January 24, 1934. 24 performances.

1934 **CHRISTIANO ZWISCHEN HIMMEL UND HOLLE** [**Christiano between Heaven and Hell.**]
5 scenes. Written by: Hans Jaray. *Première*: January 26, 1934. 15 performances.

1934 **MACBETH**
Written by: William Shakespeare. Adapted by: E. Reinhold.

1934 **DIE PRINZESSIN AUF DER LEITER** [**MEINE SCHWESTER UND ICH**] [**My Sister and I**]
2 acts. Written by: Louis Verneuil. Adapted by: Blum. *Première*: August 3, 1934. 37 performances.

1934 **SENSATIONSPROZESS [Libel]**
3 acts. Written by: Edward Wooll. *Première:* September 4, 1934. 39 performances.

1934 **EINEN JUX WILL ER SICH MACHEN**
4 acts. Written by: Johannes Nepomuk Nestroy (1842). *Première:* October 16, 1934. 35 performances.

1934 **MENSCHEN IN WEISS [Men in White]**
3 acts. Written by: Sidney S. Kingsley. *Première:* November 9, 1934. 110 performances in four theatres in Vienna.

1935 **ADRIENNE AMBROSAT**
3 acts. Written by: Georg Kaiser. *Première:* February 10, 1935. 20 performances.

1935 **EINE FRAU LUEGT**
3 acts. Written by: Fodor. *Première:* April 2, 1935. 20 performances.

1935 **DER KOENIG MIT DEM REGENSCHIRM [The King with the Umbrella]**
Musical comedy in 3 acts. Written by: Ralph Benatzky. *Première:* April 18, 1935. 104 performances, Josefstadt Theatre, Vienna. *(Preminger's second great success during his work as director at the Josefstadt Theatre, Vienna.)*

1935 **KLEINES BEZIRKS-GERICHT [The Little District Court]**
3 acts. Written by: Otto Bielen. *Première:* June 21, 1935. 63 performances.

1935 **DIE ERSTE LEGION [The First Legion]**
3 acts. Written by: Emmet Lavery. Adapted by: Schreyvogl. *Première:* October 8, 1935. 53 performances.

In the U.S.A.

1935 **LIBEL**
Drama in 3 acts. Written by Edward Wooll. Produced by: Gilbert Miller. *Première:* December 20, 1935. 159 performances, Henry Miller Theatre, N.Y.

1938 **OUTWARD BOUND**
Drama in 3 acts. Written by: Sutton Vane (1923). *Première:* December 22, 1938. 255 performances, Playhouse Company at the Playhouse, N.Y.

1939 **MARGIN FOR ERROR**
Drama in 3 acts. Written by: Clare Boothe. Produced by: Richard Aldrich and Richard Myers. *Première:* November 3, 1939. 264 performances, Plymouth Theatre, N.Y.

1940 **MY DEAR CHILDREN**
Comedy in 3 acts. Written by: Catherine Turney and Jerry Horwin. Produced by: Richard Aldrich and Richard Myers. *Première:* January 31, 1940. 117 performances, Belasco Theatre, N.Y.

1940 **BEVERLY HILLS**
Comedy in 3 acts. Written by:

Lynn Starling and Howard J. Green. Produced by: Lawrence Schwalb and Otto Preminger. 28 performances, November 1940, Fulton Theatre, N.Y.

1940 **CUE FOR PASSION**
Drama in 3 acts. Written by: Edward Chodorov and H. S. Kraft. Produced by: Richard Aldrich and Richard Myers. 12 performances, December 1940, Royale Theatre, N.Y.

1941 **THE MORE THE MERRIER**
Comedy in 3 acts. Written by: Frank Gabrielson and Irvin Pincus. Produced by: Otto Preminger and Norman Pincus. 16 performances, September 1941, Cort Theatre, N.Y.

1941 **IN TIME TO COME**
Drama with prologue and 7 scenes. Written by: John Huston and Howard Koch. Produced by: Otto Preminger. *Première:* December 28, 1941. 40 performances, Mansfield Theatre, N.Y.

1951 **FOUR TWELVES ARE 48**
Comedy in 3 acts. Written by: Joseph Kesselring. Produced by: Richard Aldrich, Richard Myers, Julius Fleischmann, Otto Preminger. 2 performances, January 1951, 48th St. Theatre, N.Y.

1951 **A MODERN PRIMITIVE**
Play by Herman Wouk. *Première.* in Hartford, Conn. No performances on Broadway. *(Preminger requested that Wouk rewrite certain scenes. When Wouk refused, Preminger decided not to present the play in N.Y.)*

1951 **THE MOON IS BLUE**
Comedy in 3 acts. Written by: F. Hugh Herbert. Produced by: Richard Aldrich, Richard Myers, Julius Fleischmann. *Première:* March 8, 1951. 924 performances, Henry Miller Theatre, N.Y.

1953 **THE TRIAL**
Opera by Gottfried von Einem. Based on *The Trial* by Franz Kafka. Presented at New York City Opera Centre, October 22 to November 1, 1953. (first production in U.S.A.)

1958 **THIS IS GOGGLE**
Play by B. Plagerman. Produced by Otto Preminger. No performances on Broadway.

1960 **CRITIC'S CHOICE**
Written by: Ira Levin. Produced by: Otto Preminger. *Première:* December 14, 1960. 189 performances, Ethel Barrymore Theatre, N.Y.

Opposite: logo for ADVISE AND CONSENT, designed by Saul Bass & Associates